Yoga for Gymnasts

Yoga for Gymnasts

BUT NOT ONLY FOR GYMNASTS

Jill Fox

ISBN: 9780692626597
ISBN: 069262659X

"It is in these little crevices of the mind and body that holds our potential, and it is our work to get to these spaces within. In there we find our gifts, our passions, and our ways."

JILL FOX

Contents

Acknowledgments xi

Chapter 1 What is Yoga 1

Chapter 2 Just Breathe 20

Chapter 3 Meditation 27

Chapter 4 Mountain Pose & Sun Salutations 33

Chapter 5 Yoga Poses 40

Chapter 6 Creating Your Very Own Yoga Practice 89

Chapter 7 Yoga for Recovery 97

Chapter 8 Calming Your Nerves 109

Chapter 9 Happy Thoughts & Intentions 112

Chapter 10 Diet & Nutrition 115

Recipes 126

Chapter 11 For the Coaches 137

About the Author 161

About the Editor 163

This book is dedicated to all walks of life. May all your footsteps be grounded, light, mindful, easy, and towards your true North....

Acknowledgments

Thank you to each beautiful yogini model-my daughter and one of my best teachers and friends, Izabel (Izzy) Fox; Katarina DelCamp (Figure Skater and 2x National Competitor); gymnasts and Foxy's Ambassadors- Emerald Gordon Wulf (contortionist, model, Toddlers & Tiaras star), Chanelle Standifer (model, Toddlers & Tiaras star) Zoey Robertson, Leighton; Athena Kohler, and Haven Koheler; Junebug's Gyms gymnasts that I have to priveledge of coaching- Luna Rezendes, Mikenzie Aribas, Reve Maguire, Bella Doolittle, Rose Pebworth, Genevieve Arzabal, Nyree Delfin, Noa Liotta, Cecile Novembre, Evelyn Guerrero, Mikayla Stanford, and Adriana Demonseot.

Thank you Foxy's Leotards, my editor and dear friend Amber Kilpatrick, ,
Matthew Koehler Photography, and Child Light Photography

CHAPTER 1

What is Yoga

"Yoga is like music. The rhythm of the body, the melody of the mind, and the harmony of the soul create the symphony of life."
—B.K.S. Iyengar

Imagine this: You're at the Olympic Games. You're suited up in your leotard and warm-ups, ready to march-out to the podium to compete. The National Anthem begins to echo through the loud speakers. The announcer is just about to announce your teams name to march out onto the floor. Your palms begin to sweat and your heart begins to beat loud and fast. The crowd is rustling and ready... My heart is beating loud and fast just thinking about it!

You see, just the thought of something triggers an emotion inside of you affecting your entire body. It's like you can physically feel as if you are some place just by thinking about it (your body barely knows the difference). Your heart starts to pump, your blood pumps faster through your veins; you may even notice your emotional or energetic levels change. Your thoughts not only can take over your physical body, but it can have way more control over your life then you ever may have thought. Through yoga, you can learn to control your thoughts which may trigger nerves or any other emotions that can interfere with your practice, gymnastics competitions, or life. You will learn how to settle butterflies (pre-competition jitters) within just a a few short breaths, calming the mind, and allowing the body to shine!

Our mind, body, and breath are all "separate" parts that work together as a whole. You could look at them like a Whol(e)y Trinity. When one of them is off, it affects all the others. When the mind takes over it can be like a broken record, for hours, days, or even years with us not even noticing. When we are lost in the mind we also are lost in the body. The mind has this sneaky way of controlling us, and we can all relate to this feeling. We can thank the mind for those times we may feel lost and tossed in the hustle & bustle of our daily lives. The racing mind can suck a lot of energy out of us.

A mind that controls us, can take us easily and gently, or sometimes very strongly, off the beaten path. To take the time to conquer your mind will be one of the most useful things you will ever do in this lifetime. One of the definitions of yoga is that it's the *science of the mind*. Yoga is way more then just yoga poses and breathing for the body. It is also strengthening for the mind and spirit. In the end, it becomes this connection the guides the champion out of us.

In The Gabby Douglas Story movie there is a great line that touches base on this trinity when coach Chow says to Gabby, "you are not separate from the skill, you are the skill. It's all ONE." Unity is actually another definition of yoga. Accessing this is what sets the champion apart from the average competitor. There is such ease to this but also such great complexity.

Yoga poses are like meditations in movement and are designed to help us rewire the connection of our mind, body, and breath so we are more able to experience this unity. If you are or were a gymnast you've probably been practicing some form of yoga all along without even realizing it. As much as yoga is similar to gymnastics though, it is also very different. Here is an example of how the two are different using a pose, which is of found in both disciplines, *the splits*:

Yoga techniques are mostly simple and subtle, but there is a lot to notice and focus on in each pose. By bringing our minds from afar back into our bodies, combined with the key focus of the breath, that is when this connection happens. This is where the magic begins to happen! The techniques can easily be forgotten though since our bodies and minds have been set on autopilot for so long, from all the patterns and habits we've picked up along the way. This is why it is important to keep up with a consistent yoga routine. Even a short amount of yoga each day is better then none at all and can help retraining your brain and resetting your autopilot.

Gymnastics Splits

You are at gymnastics practice in your splits. You are looking around the gym and talking to your teammates about something that happened in school that day. Your coach comes over and pushes your hips down. Your body tightens and your squeeze your face and bite your lip to help from screaming, "STOP!" Your mind is screaming, "when will this end?!, I've gotta get out of this, OUCH!"; your cheecks turn pink, and your heart starts racing. Your coach finallyyells, "Switch!", you take a huge sigh of relief, and you and all of your teammates switch sides.

Yoga Splits

You are in your splits, consciously breathing, focusing your eyes on one point, noticing sensations and tensions in your body as you maintain awareness and deep steady breaths. When the mind starts to take over and get noisy, you bring yourself back to the breath, back to your focal point, back to the sensations in your body, and you just stay calm and breathe. When your coach comes over to push your hips down further, this time you don't resist. You are able to be in your splits without such a mental and physical fight.

Let's take a moment: Set your timer for one minute. Close your eyes and for one minute do nothing but sit there.
Go ahead. Try it.

How did you do? Harder than it sounds, right? People in general have a hard time just sitting still with their own minds. Our minds can act as little gremlins, controlling our every step, every fear, every move. It's as if we each have a commentator in our minds that never stops talking. It's okay if your mind is talking, you just need to learn how to control the channel. You need to be in control of the dial. Through the practice of yoga you become the DJ! We are going to learn how to fix some of those broken records and clean off the dusty ole' cassettes so that your music plays a little louder and clearer.

With a little practice you will build the mental and physical strength to be able to sit for longer periods of time without feeling like you want to jump out of your skin. How long you are able to sit calm and in ease are in direct proportion to your patience and attitude you brings towards life. Think about it, if you can't sit still and be content while doing absolutely nothing, how will you be able to be calm, steady, and focused while in the hustle & bustle of everyday life, let alone during gymnastics practice? Yoga teaches us how to be still in action.

Yoga brings us to that space inside ourselves that leads us to our path, our true North. It brings you back in touch with yourself, something we easily forget by the enormous amounts of energy going outwards towards our cell phone screens. Our minds get so full of junk. But even our cell phones run out of energy after we use them for so long. In order to become fully recharged again they need to sit on a charger for a period of time to restore its' power. We too need to sit and "charge" on a conscious level, more then just sleep or rest. We need to quiet the brain down and just observe the mind. If we keep loading information, chores, duties, and tasks onto the brain without restoring it we end up walking around as robots set on autopilot.

To stay happy, healthy, and at your consistent best throughout your life, it is important to come back to your center often. Come back to *yourself* at least a little each day and eventually you will become more mindful and conscious in every given moment. Make yoga a daily ritual like brushing your teeth or taking a shower. Yoga is like your internal shower. Practicing the poses, breathing techniques, and meditations in this book will improve your gymnastics and life.

Let's go a little deeper into the history, styles, benefits, and *how-to's* of yoga......

History of Yoga

No one knows exactly how long yoga has been around exactly but it has to have been since the beginning of time. The moment Adam and Eve stepped foot on this Earth they had to have wondered, questioned, or experimented with their bodies, breaths, and minds to figure out why they came into existence. All yoga really is is *self-inquiry*. Do you ever really stop and to just think what about a miracle it is to be alive!

The body first spoke to Adam and Eve through its own language called sensation, but there was no instant verbal language that they magically spoke. Just murmurs and mumbles in the beginning. Could you imagine trying to get across what you have to say with no language existing? Language had to be spoken with their entire bodies and senses. (Two things we are becoming less in tune with everyday as technology takes over.) Imagine without all of the commotion and verbiage how clear their minds must've been. How sharp their senses must've been!

The world just keeps getting noisier, making it, or perhaps ourselves, feel chaotic, unstable, vulnerable, or out of control at times. Yoga helps to drown out some of this noisy life. It unplugs us from the outer world and plugs us back into our inner world. It shows you the path into your secret garden, just like Adam and Eve's, back to your true nature, your authentic self. You just have to be willing and allow it.

As far as to when traditional yoga was brought from the East over to the West, Swami Vivekananda was the first yogi that came over from India to help spread the peaceful message in the 1800's. Yoga didn't become mainstream or even really accepted until much later in the 1900's. People actually looked down upon it as some sort of religion or cult, which it is far from. It Is finally becoming understood by mainstream society as a good healing alternative to certain medicines. Celebrities such as Madonna and Sting started opening more interest to it in the early 90's. They were some of the first people to really grab the attention of the public into this "new-age" "body science" that was transforming the way we think and live.

I remember Madonna coming back after a break she must have taken and thinking how cool and collected she seemed. She looked so vibrant. Her muscles were strong, yet lean. She walked with new poise and confidence, and her eyes sparkled! I wanted that too. When I heard she was practicing yoga she had my attention, and many others too. People in the U.S. starting practicing yoga, and studios began popping up all over like hotcakes. Today, there are almost, if not as many, yoga studios as there are churches!

Yoga has blown up into quite the new addiction in America, and it continues to grow. People want to feel good and that's what yoga offers. Yoga studios are not the only places you will find yoga. It can now be found in hospitals, drug rehab centers, airports, corporate offices, athletic team clubs, schools, fitness clubs, rock climbing gyms, and even churches. Something very cool happens when you get a group of people together connecting to their own bodies, minds, and breaths. You can feel the unity in the room- a kind of spiritual revolution. Times they are a changing, and we know people are waking up when the messages of health and love are spreading faster then fast food chains.

The evolution of yoga continues to grow and expand, just as we do; as does our thoughts, information, and world. It is great, and necessary, to stick to the basis of yoga traditions, but just like anything, *stay open-minded* and let your own intuition and inner compass guide you. Keep your mind and heart open and your body will follow. Don't get to hung up on technicality all the time, although very important. Explore your body in different shapes and notice what and where you feel. All the answers, everything you seek is right inside of you. Listen within. Why are we always seeking elsewhere for answers, truth, and happiness?

It's like one of the old proverbs of the old lady who lost her necklace. She looked around for years and years for it and it was nowhere to be found. Then one day as she looked into the mirror, she looked hard and deep at herself and noticed the necklace was right around her neck the entire time.

Benefits of Yoga

To write all the benefits gained through yoga would be a book of its own. Each benefit has a residual affect which keeps creating more benefits. The reason yoga is so beneficial is because it gets to the root of the issues, not just to the surface as many practices or medicines may do. Yoga poses work deeper into your body then just into your tissues, bones, and joints. They go into your mental, emotional and spiritual bodies as well. Each atom, cell, and energy center are touched. Understanding that each of your bodies (physical, mental, spiritual, and even emotional) are connected, each one affecting all the other, is the first step in understanding true yoga.

Some people will notice their overall balance and alignment feeling better even after only a week of practicing yoga. Some people may notice on their very first day of practice. You will begin to eventually feel more grounded and each of your steps more sure footed. Your body will become more limber providing you with a wider range of overall motion. Your organs will function more properly radiating out a glow to your hair, skin, nails, and eyes. You will also notice, after a consistent time of practicing, that you will have less pain in your overall body and less struggle in your mind. If you get an injury, your recovery time can happen much quicker because of the increased overall agility in the body.

A consistent yoga practice is a great compliment, specifically for a gymnast's practice, for so many reasons. Gymnasts of all levels, whether you are in recreation, competitive, or on the Olympic Team, should start to include some form of yoga technique into their gymnastics practices to help improve their focus, body awareness, strength, flexibility, and more. Yoga does not put the 'wear-and-tear' on the body as other conditioning exercises may do. This is not to say replace yoga with your regular conditioning exercises, but it is an excellent addition. Yoga is also a great counter-practice to help relieve some of the mental and physical stress from the rigors of the sport.

Gymnasts have great body awareness but yoga will help you to become even more aware of your body's posture, alignment, and ability. During yoga poses bone alignment are improved and refined. This improves our gymnastics postures and skills. The bones are strengthened by using your own body's weight to put healthy stress onto your bones. This healthy stress literally deposits calcium into your bones making them stronger. This applied weight is also good for every nerve, joint, fiber, tissue, and every other part supporting your body.

Your confidence, coordination, and concentration also grow with a consistent yoga practice. You will stand taller and more sure in your body. You will be able to focus better on the present moment and certain tasks at hand. You will notice you can control your nerves better during gymnastics practices and competitions because you will have learned how to control your mind. Yoga also helps to increase blood flow to the heart and lungs bringing you a greater capacity of lung power, endurance, and stamina for your skills and routines.

These are just a few benefits of yoga. You must try it out for yourself to reap all the benefits, and after you do I would love to hear all about your journey. Message me on Instagram (@foxysleotards), or on Facebook under Foxy's Leotards, or email me at foxleotards@gmail.com. I LOVE TO TALK YOGA!

In this book you are going to learn the *how to's* to get all of the benefits of yoga right in your own home. Read on to compare the different styles...

Styles of Yoga

Yoga *is* for every body and there's no excuse because there are probably 100 different styles out there to choose from. There is sure to be a style you will find and love. I recommend trying at least a few different styles, because within each style there are also different teachers who each bring their own spice to the practice. Some teachers teach a more traditional style with no music, while others may play funky dubstep or other music in their class. Some teachers set a faster or more mellow pace to their class. Some add humor while some may be more serious. There are all styles and types out there for you to choose from. There are many different things you should expect in a yoga class. If you are new to yoga and are not certain what to expect at all in a class, I suggest walking through the door with no expectations. ☺

The style of yoga that you practice may change over time, too. We also change with the seasons so keep this in mind as you go. At times in your life you might feel as though you need a slower style, like Yin Yoga, or in the winter months you might choose a style such as Power or Hot Yoga to bring more fire and heat into your cold days. You might choose a style that is more gentle and easy on the body, like Yin or Restorative, especially if you are injured, or just to balance out your intense gymnastics training.

Remember to keep an open mind while exploring the best style of yoga that best suit you. Of the many styles of yoga available today there is sure one to suit you. We will go over the very basics of the following: *Hatha, Vinyasa, Ashtanga, Iyengar, Jivamukti, Kundalini,* and *Yin Yoga* to give you a good idea of where to begin. Each of the styles take their own special path but they all lead to the same blissful state so listen to your instincts and pick what's right for *you*.. From the following brief descriptions of the 7 styles of yoga listed you will have a good idea of which might best fit you.

Try one, try all! ☺

Hatha Yoga

Hatha yoga is one of the oldest forms of documented yoga. In the 15th century, Yogi Swatmarama introduced *Hatha* in India. Most styles of yoga rooted from hatha. *Hatha* has been said to mean sun and moon. This sun and moon energy are meant to unify and balance the male and female energies inside of each of us. The utmost goal in Hatha yoga is relating to the body in poses, which helps bring you deeper into your subtle energy bodies, which in turn leads to meditation. Meditation is the main goal in hatha yoga.

The practice is slow and the poses are focused on individually rather than in a flow or in a sequence of poses. It is designed and practiced to help align all parts of the body, mind, muscles, skin, and bones. *Hatha* can be used to describe any type of physical yoga. The physical practice of yoga is designed to prepare our bodies for deep meditation. In fact, poses were created to help the traditional yogi to sit in meditation longer without the body cramping up or getting stiff.

Most people have probably practiced some form of hatha yoga. If you've done a downward dog before you've done some form of hatha yoga! If you were to go to a Hatha yoga class you should expect the classes to be fairly mellow. There may be light music playing in the back round. You will be challenged but will not sweat like you would in a Vinyasa or Bikram class. If you go pose by pose in this book then you will be practicing Hatha Yoga.

In fact, if you've never done yoga before, this might be a good style for you to start with to help you get acquainted with the general yoga poses. Start by picking out the poses from this book that call to you and try them, after reading the chapters on Breath, Mountain, and Meditation. Using all of the yoga principles from those chapters will prepare you for the poses.

Vinyasa Yoga

Vinyasa literally means, "to flow". In a *Vinyasa* class you will probably hear the teacher say, "take a *Vinyasa*". This will connects a poses and helps to build strength and stamina. It is not always required to take the vinyasa every time a teacher says it in a class. If you can maintain a deep steady breath, then keep doing the vinyasas, but if they start to lose the steadiness of breath eliminate some of the vinyasas. The breath is synchronized with the flow, so keep it smooth and steady.

The three poses that make up a vinyasa link together a series of additional yoga poses in a Vinyasa class. The vinyasas create heat in the body helping the body to open and expand. In a Vinyasa yoga class you should expect, most likely, music to be playing. The students in the classes usually consist of a range from younger to older. The sequences will most likely be different every class since the teachers have a little more free range to make up their own flows and sequences. Vinyasa yoga is less rigid then some other styles and allows the body more freedom to move in a fluid way.

The body during the poses expands and lengthens on the inhales and folds or contracts on the exhales. The movement between the body and breath become dance-like with the breath being the lead partner, beginning a millisecond before the body follows. Moving in this way creates a calming and healing affect on the entire mind and body. It also helps to move tension (which is just another way of saying *stuck energy*), and it releases physical, mental, and emotional toxins from the body.

Let's go over a complete vinyasa with some modifications. Get familiar with vinyasas by practicing a few rounds using the guide on the following page. If you are new to yoga, modify with the knees down and use Cobra instead of Up Dog. As you progress and get stronger you can then lift your knees during Chatturanga, and replace Cobra with Up-Dog.

A Vinyasa is a series of the following 3 poses:

1. Chatturanga- a push up with elbows back (on or off knees)

2. Up-Dog (or cobra pose)

3. Down-Dog (an upside-down "V")

Ashtanga Yoga

Ahhh, *Ashtanga*... This is a classical style of yoga. Patthabi Jois (1915-2009), from Mysore India, is the "guru" who is most commonly associated with *Ashtanga* yoga. *Ashtanga* Yoga is broken down as "Eight-Limb Path"-

There are 4 parts of Asthanga yoga:

1. The Opening Sequence
2. 1 of 6 Sequences-
   a. Primary Series
   b. Intermediate Series
   c. Advanced Series A
   d. Advanced Series B
   e. Advanced Series C
   f. Advanced Series D
3. Back-Bend Sequences
4. Inverted and Finishing Sequences

The practice takes anywhere from one to two hours and is meant to be practiced everyday, except during moon cycles for women, or on a full moon for anyone. Ashtanga yoga is a very disciplined style of yoga and can take months or even years to advance to just the Intermediate Series. Some people may never even advance to the Advanced Series because the poses are so challenging. Even if you never make it to the Advanced Series though, there are many benefits to just the Primary Series alone.

The beauty of Ashtanga is the routine is always the same so it is easy to track your progress, get on your mat, and go. This is often how an elite gymnast will warm up- the same warm up routine each day. Finding a good repetitive warm up is wise. Repetition is key for improving your gymnastics. Gymnasts will perform any where from 10-20 routines a day, up to 7 days a week preparing for big competitions such as the Olympics.

In an Ashtanga yoga class you should expect the opening prayer, or chant, then a teacher guides the Primary Series with option for Mysore, where students who already know the sequence can practice at their own pace. So both beginner and advanced Ashtangi's practice together in the same room. It becomes a more individualized practice by how the teacher gives the students more personalized adjustments and instructions. You will most likely not hear music in an Ashtanga yoga class.

Eight-Limb Yoga Path

1. Yamas
2. Niyamas
3. Asana
4. Pranayama
5. Pratyahara
6. Dharana
7. Dhyana
8. Samadhi

1. Yamas:
   a. ahimsa- non-violence, harming no one
   b. satya- truthfulness; no lying, gossiping, or verbal abuse
   c. asteya- non stealing, taking only what's given to you
   d. brahmacharya- living in harmony with all things
   e. aparigraha- greedlessness

2. Niyamas:
   a. shauca- cleanliness in hygiene and thought
   b. santosha- contentment; free of anger or desire
   c. tapas- self discipline
   d. svadhyaya- study of self through text and inner work
   e. ishvarpranidhana- opening to a higher power

3. Asana: the poses

4. Pranayama: breath control

5. Pratyahara: turn senses inward

6. Dharana: concentration

7. Dhyana: meditation

8. Samadhi: union with higher power

8 limbs of yoga
8.samadhi
7.dhyana
6. dharana
5. pratyahara
4. pranayama
3. asana
1. yamas-how you relate to others
2. niyamas-how you relate to yourself

Iyengar Yoga

B.K.S. Iyengar is the founder of *Iyengar* Yoga, and his style is also firmly based on the 8-Limb Path of yoga. There is little to no flow in these classes, and each pose is held a little longer; often times using props such as belts, straps, or blocks. Props were actually introduced to other styles of yoga through Iyengar' style.

The use of props is great because they help to support your body in posture so you can focus more on the most important part of the practice, the breath. B.K.S. stressed the importance of the breath. In fact, he even wrote an entire book on the breath called Light on Pranayama.

If you were to go to an Iyengar style yoga class you should expect an older crowd. The slower pace that pays more attention to detail in comfortable and very beneficial for the aging body. The teacher will probable not be playing music but may weave a story through the class. You will feel challenged physically by the poses and mentally by the stillness in the poses. Poses can be held for up to 30 breaths! This gives you time to feel and explore areas of your body you may not usually pay attention to. Sometimes this slower pace can be just as, if not more, beneficial to become centered in the body.

There are *200 different poses* and *14 different breathing* exercises in *Iyengar style yoga*. It is a great style of yoga for gymnasts and athletes to practice because its key focus is alignment, and alignment is of utmost importance when it comes to a gymnast's skills and performance. Alignment helps a gymnast to balance better on the beam, swing better on bars, tumble and dance better and floor, and have more power on vault. Not only is alignment in the body vital on so many levels for a gymnast, but also in the mind; two things a gymnast *must* conquer to excel in the sport, physical and mental balance. These are two things *any* person must have in order to excel in *anything*!

Try to keep what you do on a daily basis aligned with your dreams and goals. We don't have to look at it as just physical alignment. Yoga helps us to think outside of the box and realize life is all connected. Align your visions with your actions. Align your words with what you mean. Your life will then begin to align with your heart.

Jivamukti Yoga

Jivamukti is a beautiful style of yoga developed by Sharon Gannon and David Life. They are a couple in New York who designed this amazing style of yoga in 1986. "Jiva" in Hindi means "soul of a living being". "*Mukti*" means salvation. *Jivamukti* can be translated to mean, "liberation while living". Do you truly feel liberated? David and Sharon's belief is to do no harm to any beings, or the planet, so they follow a very strict vegan lifestyle. Not only do they not consume anything that has harmed an animal, but they won't even wear clothing, shoes, or accessories made from animal by-products. *Jivamukti* is a vigorous physical and intellectual style of Hatha Yoga. It has a strong foundation in the ancient spiritual traditions of yoga with a fun upbeat spice. It is meant to be practiced to improve our relationships with everything. It is a path to enlightenment through compassion for all beings.

In a Jivamukti Yoga class, you can expect to hear music. Music is a big part of the class so you will always hear it in a yoga classroom. The beats are usually funky, fun, and modern. Don't be surprised if you hear Snoop Dog, Beastie Boys, or some other unexpected song! The teacher will usually tie in some sort of theme or story into their class. Jivamukiti draws a wide range of ages, but you won't find this style everywhere. The trainings are very intense and you are expected to live the vegan lifestyle. This may be a reason why it is not as commonly found. There are an abundance of yoga teachers and most don't go through such extreme diet and clothing changes, all go through major spiritual and mental changes.

Sthira and sukham are two Hindi words commonly used in *Jivamukti*. Sthira means to be fully engaged; it means the ability to hold strong, steady, and stable in mind, body, and soul. Sukham means comfort, ease, light, surrender, or self-acceptance. In Jivamukti, the goals of the poses are sthira and sukham. To put it very simply-*Strength and Surrender*. We want to be strong and active in our poses, but at the same time we also want to be calm and relaxed.

The Jivamukti chant (that you will always hear in class) goes like this:

Lokah Samastah Sukhino Bhavantu

(sounds like (low-ka-some-a-sta-sue-key-no-ba-va-n-two)

May all beings everywhere be happy and free, and may the thoughts, words, and actions of my own life contribute in some way to that happiness and to that freedom for all.

***Chanting simply helps to focus your mind and help bring it into meditation.*

There are 5 disciplines in Jivamukti Yoga:

1. Ahimsa- to not injure or harm any being or thing. Jivamukti's follow a strict vegan lifestyle in which no animals are killed or harmed for their food or clothing.

2. Bhakti- means devotion. Jivamukti's believe without devotion a pose is meaningless.

3. Meditation- the practice of letting go (of bad habits or tendencies.)

4. Nada- deep listening development using music or words.

5. Shastra-ancient yogic scripture and chanting.

Kundalini Yoga

Kundalini means "coiled snake". According to yogic tradition, *Kundalini* is a divine energy that sits at the base of the spine and coils around the sacrum three and a half times. We are all born with this energy and *Kundalini* yoga is practiced to access it through our own inner efforts. *Kundalini* was once a secret practice amongst certain elite because there was belief that the public could not handle the powers the practice gave them. In 1968, *Yoga Bhajan*, Kundalini master, claimed that is everyone's birthright to tap into our God given gifts and the practice slowly became more accessible to the public. The practice is now available to everyone, but it is still not as common as some of the other styles of yoga you find in studios today.

Kundalini Yoga is considered the most sacred of all styles because its main focus is spiritual awakening and connection to the Higher Self. Although, all styles of yoga lead to this *higher* awakening of consciousness. It is something that will not be able to be helped. You will for sure be touched and changed on some level if yoga becomes a practice that you learn and incorporate daily, even if for as little as 5 minutes a dayl

In a Kundalini yoga class you can expect to hear some mellow music in the background, but not always. Chanting often opens the class using the call-response method, which is where the teacher recites each line at a time and the student follows. This technique is great for learning and remembering the chants. The classes are slower, but challenging, and have poses such as holding your arms over your head for 5 minutes! You may find more surprises in a Kundalini class such as breaking out into a free flowing dance, or incorporating different breathing techniques. You will focus more on your subtle energy bodies during the poses. A story of theme is often weaved into class. The teacher usually wears all white, representing purity. Yogi Bhajan, believed a person's aura transmitted even further by wearing all white. Awakening to the Self happens in Kundaiini through all the elements listed below.

The practice consists of:

1. Mantras- repeated words
2. Pranayama- breath control
3. Chakras- energy centers along spine
4. Bandhas- body "locks"
5. Kriyas- repeated actions
6. Asanas- pose

Yin Yoga

You've probably seen a yin & yang symbol before. *Yin* is the lighter (or cool) side, and yang is the darker (or hot) side. *Yin* Yoga is an exceptionally slow style of yoga. In a typical class you may only practice just a few poses and each is held anywhere from five to twenty minutes. *Yin* yoga targets "yin" areas (smaller, harder to get to) of the body, such as the joints, tendons, ligaments, deep facial tissues, and smaller bones. This is a great style of yoga for anyone, but especially for an injured gymnast or someone in recovery.

Since the poses are held longer, you are able to reach into deeper levels of the body, even energetically. Going this deep in the body gets into dusty places of your body that haven't been visited in awhile, and quite possibly ever, so don't be surprised if going in deep like this brings up some emotional stuff for you later that day or even week. Yoga is like dusting off the layer of dust on a mirror. Once it's clean your are able to see your reflection much clearer.

Don't plan on breaking a sweat in Yin yoga. In fact you will probably want to wear long sleeves and pants, and possibly even socks during class to help keep your body warm. You don't want to be cold while practicing yoga. This will tighten up your muscles and you want your muscles relaxed. Lots of props are used and encouraged for extra support while practicing yin poses. Most likely the teacher will be playing slow gentle music in the yoga classroom.

Much of the benefits from this practice come from the extra time in the poses and slowing way down to pay close attention to details you might have missed by not holding a pose for so long. Being able to breathe and stay calm in the idleness can be challenging but also a great way to build your brain muscle and patience. People are wired to react quickly and get out of a difficult situation as quick as possible. In yoga we feel sometimes uncomfortable sensations and our instinct is to get out. Yin yoga helps to bring clarity and stillness to the chaos. Yin yoga helps to bring a balance into our lives. From balancing our up and down energy and moods, to our mind, body, and soul. Yin is a great counter practice if you lead a high intensity lifestyle.

Tips to Begin Yoga

If you are reading this you are ready to begin! That's part of the beauty of yoga- absolutely nothing is needed to begin. Even if you don't have a yoga mat you can still practice. Simply grab a towel or blanket, or just use your carpet. In India, yogis would practice on the cement, so no excuses. Believe it or not, you don't even need any of the fancy yoga pants! Clear enough space for yourself and wear comfortable clothing. All you need is your breath, an open mind, and the willingness to have patience with yourself.

Let your practice happen gradually and naturally. You will need to put effort in but never use force. Accept yourself from where you are right her and right now. Are you coming back from an injury? Do you have incredibly tight muscles and joints from heavy tumbling and conditioning? You could be someone who has a very difficult time focusing or sitting still. Maybe you are a gymnast who is letting your fear and nerves take over and need some help and encouragement. Any place you are in is perfect. We all will be coming from a different place and that's where we begin.

Wherever you are today, this book will help guide you so you will be able to develop a home yoga practice that suits you; a practice that you can do in the comforts of your own home. Practicing yoga will help you gain more control and focus as a gymnast and as a person. It will also keep you primed and focused in between gymnastics practices. Customize and modify things in this book as needed. There are no rules. Use the poses and the practice to help you discover more about yourself and your potential.

Try out different styles of yoga to see what resonates with you like most. Even try going to a yoga studio for a class sometime. Whatever you do, don't stop trying yoga until you find the style you love. There is a style for you. It might seem hard or boring at first, but stay with it. Take some time to re-train your mind and reset your autopilot. I promise, you will notice an incredible difference in your gymnastics training, your performance, and in your life.

Before you begin any of the poses in this book, make sure you've at least read Chapter 2 first, *The Breath.* The breath is going to be your main focus in all poses. Once you learn more about how and why the the breath is so important, it will become one of your best friends. You won't believe it's been right there with you all along just waiting to be given attention If there is one thing you take from this book may it be that you understand the power of the breath. Let's get right to it!.

Now, take a deep breath.... Inhale- 4 counts/ Exhale- 4 counts.....

CHAPTER 2

Just Breathe

"All things share the same BREATH- the beast, the tree, the man. The air shares its spirit with all of the life it supports."
CHIEF SEATTLE

Breathing is one thing that every single being, flower, insect, flower, fish, Mother Earth and Ocean all share. We all pulse to the same rhythm by connecting to the breath from the second we are born into the world. Your breath is as close to you as anything will ever be. Breathing happens organically and you never have to remind yourself to do it. Although in very intense situations it can sometimes feel like you have to remind yourself to breathe. Your breath holds a special key, and once you find it you will be able to unlock doors you never knew you even had.

By learning to control the breath we begin to gain control of the mind, and in turn more physical and emotional control in our lives as well. *Your breath is the bridge between your mind and body.* Your thoughts run along your breath. Keep the breath steady and smooth and you will notice your mind more calm. This act alone can start to train your mind to surf along the smaller, more steady waves rather than the Big Kahunas. Next time your feel nervous or anxious stop for a moment and notice what your breath is doing. Is it more then likely shallow and quick?

The breath is like your compass in each of the poses. It will guide you into mental stillness, and let you know while in your poses if you've gone in too far or not far enough. If you lose your deep steady breaths that means you've come to far into the pose and you just need to back out a bit. You want to keep a deep steady breath your entire practice. No stress or strain on the breath. Build and grow the poses patiently followed by the stable breath as opposed to growing the breath while in a deeper pose.

Keeping the focus on the breath for a long period of time can be challenging. At first, you will notice your mind quickly taking back over once it recognizes its lost its' control, and all of the sudden you've totally forgotten you were even focusing on the breath. With time and practice your focus will improve and you will be able to focus for longer and longer. The noisy mind will slowly lose its' power. This also becomes helpful in breaking any bad habits you may have. Admit it. We all have them! By shifting the patterns of your brain, even in the smallest way, you will notice many changes in both your body and your life.

Our brains are much like computers imputing data at a very high speed. When we have too much data in our computers our hard drives can eventually crash, just like our brains. In order for our computers to run efficiently we need to empty the trash and organize our files regularly. Meditation is like emptying the garbage in our brains. We will discuss more about meditation in the following chapter, but let's continue with the breath since that's what will essentially get you to that state of meditation.

Breath Patterns

Ancient yogis believed that we were only granted so many breaths per lifetime. Breath techniques were used to slow down their breathing in order to prolong theirs lives. Some yogis have been known to get their breathing down to only 1 breath per minute! (That's a 30 second inhale and 30 second exhale!) Could you imagine if we really were given only so many breaths per life? Each breath would be so sacred.

About 90% of our energy comes from the way we breathe. You could instantly access over 50% more of your energy by just changing the way you breathe. Most people only access about 10-20% of their full capacity of breath because it is too fast, and/or the nostrils/nadis (keep reading- *nadis* will be explained ☺) are clogged. We typically breathe around 20 unconscious breaths per minute, but this is way more than we are designed to breathe. We should only be breathing between 10-12 breaths per minute.

You have over 6,000 miles of nerves in your body and they are all affected by the rhythm of your breath. This is why a steady breath is so important for your overall health. Imagine the difference your nerves feel along your inhales and exhales- either choppy or smooth. Which wave do you want your thoughts riding on? The sooner you grasp the idea of just how powerful and important it is to keep a quality breath, the better your life will be. You will have the ability to feel a new way in your mind and body almost instantly just by learning and applying a few breathing techniques to your life.

Let's take a moment and just notice the breath: Set your timer for 1 minute and sit in a comfortable position. Notice your breathing. Is it fast or slow; shallow or deep; smooth or quivery? Just notice...

If your breaths were short and quick, you may have noticed that your heart was beating faster, or if your breaths were slower you may have noticed you felt pretty calm. You may have had a hard time noticing the breath at all because your mind may have kept taking over. We can actually manipulate our breathing patterns to slow down the mind. We can speed up our breathing to stimulate the mind and body if we need more energy, or we can slow down our breathing if we want to relax. We can even change our body temperate with our breath. Speed it up for more heat or use the cooling breath to cool down. To control the breath is called pranayama. Prana is the breath (energy), and Yama means to control. We have the control of our breath and this control is the first step into your inner world which connects us to a very powerful source.

You have thousands of (energetic) channels, called nadis (in Sanskrit) that run through your body that you can think of as tiny rivers. There is a main channel going down the middle of your spine called the Sushumna Channel, that you can imagine as a waterfall. All channels lead to this main channel. Some channels are bigger and some are smaller, but all of them (rivers) need to keep a steady flow towards Sushumna (waterfall) in order for your best physical and mental health (abundance).

When even one little channel is clogged, this affects every other channel. Channels can be blocked from things such as physical tension (stuck energy), emotional baggage, toxins from thoughts or outside sources such as pollution or pesticides. The poses help to move the energy from the outside-in, and the breath helps to move the energy from the inside-out. Our fullest potential lies deep within each of these rivers. When the rivers are flowing rapidly, this is when we are fully engaged and the champion inside of us comes out.

The most common type of pranayama in yoga is Ujjayi Pranayama. This style of breath is mostly used in most yoga classes. It means "victorious" breath. Ujjayi breathing creates an oceanic sound in the back of the glottis (back of the throat). The vibration from the breath creates a nice inner-vibration and massage for the organs, nerves, muscles, and tendons around your throat and neck. It is soothing for the brain and helps to quiet the mind.

Let's take a moment and try Ujjayi Pranayama: Hold one hand in front of your mouth about 5 inches away, palm facing towards you and imagine your hand is a window. Inhale through your nose with your lips slightly sealed, and as you exhale open your mouth and fog the window. You should be making the sound "Hhaaaaaaa" as you breath out. Do this a few times. Now, lower your hand back down and do the exact same breathing but keep the lips slightly sealed on the exhales, too. You should feel a vibration in your glottis (back of your throat).

Pranayama Exercises

You might have heard of people "glowing" after a yoga class. When all of your nadis are open the energy extends beyond your skin, creating a glowing aura around you. Pranayama is an essential ingredient in yogic discipline. It creates not only physical and emotional changes but subtle chemical changes in the body. The respiratory and circulatory systems are improved, memory is improved, the brain becomes stronger, and many other benefits are gained. It is even linked to a happier and more positive attitude and life.

Like yoga, there are lots of styles and techniques for pranayama to choose from. Following is a list of 5 more practices that you can experiment with and hopefully find one that you can do for at least 1-2 minutes everyday. You can do while brushing your teeth, walking between classes at school, or winding down for bed at night. Be patient with yourself and keep an open mind. Even master yogis found the breath work to be straining at first. Remember repetition is key. Practice, practice, practice even if only 5 minutes a day. Always keep it light and enjoyable and adding more as you feel called. Be persistent. Yoga takes discipline.

*Belt/Strap Feedback

This is an excellent exercise where you can actually feel the breath as your lungs press up against the belt. The belt acts as great feedback helping you become aware of how big or shallow your breath is. Having the belt around the ribs gives you a force to work with, and can also help you remember to keep your awareness on the breath. *Here's what to do:*

1. Start in a comfortable seated position, preferably on a bolster or blanket so that your hips are just slightly higher then our knees.
2. Secure the belt around the lowest part of your ribcage. It should fit tight enough so that you don't have to hold it up on the exhale, but loose enough so that you can get a nice full inhale.
3. Start your timer for 3 minutes and work up to more time as you improve. Pay attention to the steady, equal rhythms of the inhales and exhales.
4. After the 3 minutes, take off the belt and continue to breathe regularly for another minute.

*Nadi Sodhana

Think of a time when you had a cold or allergies and your nose was all stuffed up. Both nostrils are attached to the Sushumna Channel, our main energy channel that we just covered. If either of the nostrils is clogged, even just a little, you instantly lose a significant amount of energy. Remember, 90% of our energy comes from how we breathe! Nadi Shodhana is a technique of breathing to help us clear and open up the nostrils for the breath to run through freely. You may notice immediate results after only a few minutes!

Nadi is a tubular organ that transports energy in the body. The body is filled with thousands of nadis.
Sodhana means to purify or cleanse.
Here's what to do:

1. Start in a comfortable seated position, preferably on a bolster or blanket so that your hips are just slightly higher then your knees. Lower your chin slightly, lift your chest and heart upwards as your pull your lower ribcage down and in.
2. Rest your left hand to your left knee and bring your right hand up to your face. Your "peace sign" fingers of your right hand will be together and go right between your brows. Your ring and little finger (together) will rest gently over your left nostril, and your thumb will be rest gently over your right nostril.
3. Press your thumb to your right nostril to block any air flow and exhale through your left nostril.
4. Inhale through your left nostril.
5. Press down on the left nostril now to block any air flow, and release the press on the right nostril.
6. Inhale through the right nostril.
7. Cover right nostril.
8. Exhale through left nosril.
9. Continue for up to 20 rounds.

*Cooling Breath

The cooling breath is great for when your body feels overheated, for instance, during gymnastics conditioning. It is like a built-in air conditioner and you can access it on the first breath. This breath is also how dogs and many other animals breathe to cool down. The cooling breath is also great to relax the central nervous system so try a few during practice or competition when you're feeling the "heat". It's super simple, and breathing in this way can instantly cool you off. Traditional yogis believed practicing this breath would keep you young and attractive. *Here's what to do:*

1. Start in a comfortable seated position, preferably on a bolster or blanket so that your hips are just slightly higher then our knees.
2. Stick out your tongue and roll it, sides of the tongue upwards. Make your lips into the small shape of an "o".
3. Inhale for 4 counts through the tongue.
4. Close your lips and hold all of the air in. 5. Exhale for 6 counts out your nose.
6. Repeat.
7. Notice the cooling feeling.

*Lion's Breath

This wonderful breath may feel extremely awkward at first because your tongue is sticking out and eyes look like they are popping. It only takes 1 or 2 breaths to feel the affects from it. It is great for relieving tension, mentally or physically, so you can do a few throughout your day as needed. *Lion's Breath* is also known to help aid sore throats, bad breath, and other respiratory blockages. Also try this breath while in poses, especially in backbends to help open up more channels in your body. *Here's how it's done:*

1. Begin sitting in a comfortable position, either on your seat, a chair, or preferably on your knees. Sit up tall like a lion.
2. Place your arms straight in front of you, hands on your knees, fingers straight and pointing out, slightly downwand, and spread wide.
3. Inhale as you press your palms down and puff out your chest.
4. Exhale and you stick out your tongue and open your eyes as wide as possible.
5. Inhale through your nose slowly and continue for up to 10 breaths.

*Breath of Fire (Kapalabhati)

Kapalabhati literally translates to "skull shining". It can be a great warm-up to other pranayama exercises. The forceful exhales help to move any stale air from the body. It is great for the digestive system, heart, liver, and more. The stomach gets toned. The sinuses are cleansed, and the brain is also nourished (since it lies directly behind the nostrils.) *Kapalabhati* breathing is mostly practiced in Kundalini yoga. Here's how it's done:

1. Begin sitting in a comfortable position, either on your seat, a chair, or on your knees.
2. Place your hands on your knees with straight arms, and take a big inhale through your nose, filling up your abdomen. The inhale should be silent and long.
3. To exhale, draw the abdomen sharply in and up, drawing the air quickly out of your lungs.
4. Focus on the rhythm: exhale, exhale, exhale...*Exaggerate* the exhale
5. The inhales happen quickly and effortlessly in between the exhales from the force of the belly drawing in.

Whatever technique you are practicing you will be okay if you do just one thing, remember to breathe! ☺

CHAPTER 3

Meditation

"Meditation can reintroduce you to the part that's been missing."
RUSSELL SIMMONS

You could be the strongest person in the world, but if your mind is not in control what good does all that strength do? When we meditate, it is like crunches for the brain. Our mental muscle grows stronger. Meditation helps us to quiet the loud chatter in the mind so that the brain can communicate with the body more fully. The brainwaves have time to function properly giving your body and mind a feeling of calmness and control.

Physical and mental exhaustion can both be equally draining. Mental activity robs from our physical energy, and as athletes this is a big deal breaker. We have to learn to harness our thoughts and keep the mind in the body, in every muscle, in every bone, in every move, especially during training, or a competition. That thought power is the sustaining juice that creates and sustains champions.

Meditation is a solution. It is a valuable, free source, which we have available to us at all times- just like the breath. It's always there and waiting for us to notice. Meditation techniques have even been known to help cure eating disorders, neurological issues, depression, anxiety, and more. The benefits are another book of its own but can only truly be understood by trying for yourself.

Yoga poses were originally practiced to prepare the body to be able to sit longer in meditation. Meditation can be more challenging then some of the actual yoga poses because our minds are like wild animals that just want to run loose. Training the mind can be much like training a puppy. Jack Kornfield, one of my favorite meditation teachers, describes it perfectly. Our mind is just like the puppy that wants to run around and play all day, and we have to keep reminding and swaying it back. With consistent practice, the mind will come back quicker and quicker, and may eventually begin to stay put.

Adam Levine, who also practices yoga, said it perfectly on The Voice one time, "nothing gets you more off track then your head." It is so true. You need to learn to control the mind before it consumes you. It can consume you with you not even noticing. In the hustle & bustle of today's world it is easy to get swallowed up. Meditation is another key to keeping you calm and focused. It will help you build the concentration and mindfulness you need to succeed, not only in gymnastics, but in life. Success in this book means to live a life free from stress, worry, aches, and pains in body, mind, or soul.

Sitting in stillness helps to center and ground us. Use each of your senses to help drop into this new quieted mind- *feel* your breath, your clothing against your skin, and the ground below you. *Smell* the aromas around you. *Listen* to those subtle noises around you: the birds, breath, static electricity in the room, quieting buzzing. Bringing your awareness to parts of your body and subtleties around you will helps your mind to lose grip and allows blissful and potential energy from within you to submerge. Let's go deeper....

Beginning to Meditate

Coming to your mat, chair, bolster, or wherever you are sitting can be one of the hardest parts of meditating. Inspiring yourself enough to get to your seat will be half the battle. Once you get past that "runners high" your will not want to come out!

1. Relax the best you can and make sure you are completely comfortable. Adjust until you are.
2. Root your seat bones down equally.
3. Imagine your spine is an antennae reaching up towards the sky.
4. Draw your belly button in slightly and draw your low ribs in and down.
5. Lift your heart slightly and relax your shoulders down.
6. Your chin is parallel to the Earth and facial muscles are soft.
7. Look into the 3rd eye (space between brow), with your eyes soft or closed.
8. Breathe. Repeat, repeat, repeat...

If you are totally new to meditating, know that it takes awhile to get the hang of it. At first it may feel as if there is no point to just "sitting there". But hang in there. It takes a lot of self-discipline to do it on your own so if you do not have a teacher or group to hold you accountable expect even more patience with yourself. A good way to build stamina to sit for longer periods of time is to start with 1-minute on day 1 and add 1 minute a day for 30 days. It's a great challenge and if you find at least one other person to join the challenge with you, you'll be more likely to complete it by holding each other accountable.

The mind is going to wander naturally. The point of meditation practice is not to have a mind with nothing going on. The mind is going to constantly fluctuate. That's just what it does. We just don't want it to fluctuate so high and so low. We can make those waves less intense. The point of meditation practice is to be able to take the reigns of the mind when it gets out of control; to call the puppy back when he is wandering around aimlessly. We can practice harnessing the mind and bringing it back to a more controlled state in several different ways. Mantras, malas, and imagery can all aid in centering the mind.

Mantra

Mantras are a string of words, sounds, and syllable, repeated over and over to help direct the mind to a more stable condition. They are like affirmations helping to enforce a more positive outlook in life. Mantra literally means, "instrument of thought". The words can be short and simple, or entire chants, such as LOKAH SAMASTAH SUKHINO BHAVANTU.

Simple mantras, such as *I AM* and *LET GO*, are great to repeat in your head as you inhale and exhale. For instance as you inhale recite quietly to yourself the word *let*, and as you exhale recite to yourself the word *go*. Use one of these or make up your own simple matra that resonates with you. This is a simple meditation to help you begin if you are new to meditating. It is also great for the advanced practitioner. Mantras redirect the noisy mind and send signals to the brain to help you relax.

Bija mantras are one-syllable sounds associated with each of your 7 Chakras. By chanting the bija mantra associated with each Chakra you can activate its' energy. Chakras are like spiritual glands, each one associated with a different (physical) organ and (spiritual) area in your life.

Starting from the bottom and going up towards the crown of the head, the Bija Mantras are: *LAM, VAM, RAM, YAM, HAM, OM, OM*. You can focus on one Chakra at a time and repeat the bija sound associated with it; or go up along the Chakras one at a time, with your minds eye, saying the sound for each Chakra as you come to it, and recite the entire mantra. Repeat for 10 minutes for an all over body and mind massage.

(Color in the picture below with the corresponding colors for yet another meditation. Muladhara=red, Svadhisthana=orange, Manipura=yellow, Anahata=green, Vishudha=blue, Ajna=indigo, Sahasrara=no color (white light). (Did you know coloring counts as meditation?!)

Mala

Malas consist of a strand of *108* beads and help to aid your mind into concentration. During practice you can recite a mantras, bija mantras, or simply counts while passing over each bead with your fingers. The mind is trained in this way to focus on one task at a time.

This meditation is done by holding the strand of beads gently in your right hand with your middle and index finger. Starting with the largest bead, you will gently guide each bead, one by one, towards you with your thumb as you say your mantra of choice, or count. Once you come to the biggest bead again, you know you have done a full cycle. If you want to begin again, reverse the direction as you count the beads again.

A mala resembles a necklace and you can easily make one with any kind of beads. Little round beads are recommended since they run along the fingers nicely. Carry your mala in your gym bag and bring it to meets or practice to remind yourself to stay calm. You can also wear your mala around your neck or wrap it around your wrist as a simple reminder.

Follow this diagram to help you build your own mala:

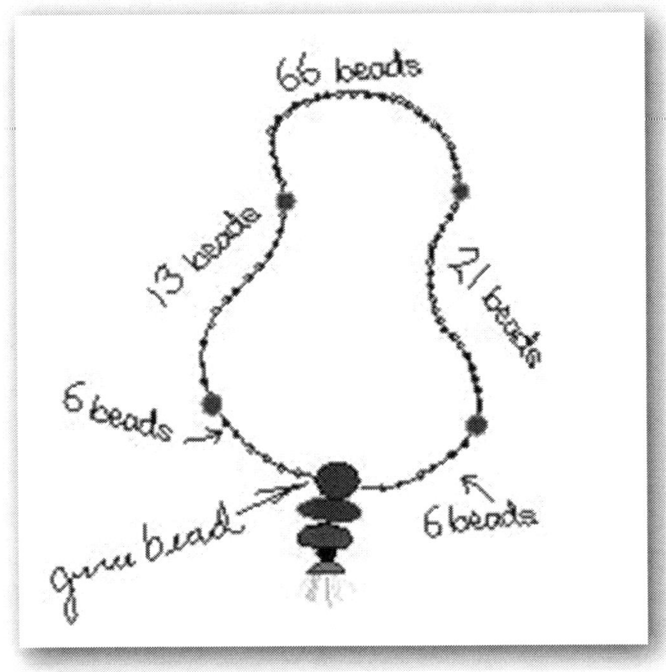

Imagery

You've probably done some form of meditation before without even knowing it. Most gymnasts probably have already practiced some form of imagery. Imagining yourself doing your routines or skills perfectly, over and over, is one of the most powerful things that you can do to help improve your gymnastics. The body may actually feel as if it is really doing the routine and this feeling may be stored in your muscle memory.

In *imagery*, whatever it is that you are wanting, a perfect routine, a new career, stronger muscles, you have to do is act as if you already that. You want to be able to feel it in your bones; picture every last detail of your dream. Leave a lasting impression in your body and mind about your dreams and goals. Imagery is the very thing that sets successful people apart from others. Most people just wish they could do or have something and it doesn't go much further then that because they don't fully believe they are capable of getting it. Successful people 'imagine' what they want, they believe it, and they allow it, no doubt or questions asked.

As you imagine yourself doing your perfect routines use as much detail as possible. The more the better. Feel the leather of the beam under your feet as your feet firmly plant, feel the elastic of your leotard hugging your body as you move; smell the chalk and sweat in the arena; hear the music in the air and the crowd in the background; feel your feet sticking to the soft mat and landing each dismount perfectly. When your routine is done, see the judges flashing your perfect 10.0. Before bed is the best time to do this type of imagery. Right before sleep is when your mind goes in and takes over the body for the entire rest of the night. This transition time is vital and should be kept positive and stress-free. This is the time to think of the things you want to attract, not bumming or stressing about the things your don't have.

If you want perfect Tkachev's, as you fall asleep at night envision yourself: grips on, bars chalked, and already set to the perfect setting; giants feeling powerful as the bars slightly creak as you tap-swing through. You hear your teammates cheering you on as your toes come up and you release the bar at the perfect moment! Fly over the bar, in the air you see the bar, and grab it dead on! Maybe it's more simple: you want your splits. See your legs straight, back knee turned under, front leg extended and toes pointed. Your chest is up and your hips and legs are down to the floor into your perfect split. You got this. Whatever it is you want, it is yours. Believe it and go for it!

Savasana

Savasana is found at the end of all yoga classes and can range anywhere from 2-20 minutes or more. The word *savasana* literally means "corpse pose". We let go any control of the breath or movement of the body and try to completely surrender your physical body. The goal of the pose is just to let everything go and become an observer of what goes on.

Letting go in this way can be quite hard at first because we were always taught to not relax, but when learned to do properly, this can be one of the most beneficial things you will ever do. When the body stops moving the mind starts to creep in again. When the mind is noisy we get uncomfortable and want to move the body to distract it. Notice this sometimes when you are tossing and turning in bed at night.

During yoga poses you will notice your mind is quieter. It is focused on each body part, the breath, and all the details of each pose. When the body comes into stillness and the body get to fully relax, the mind may begin to seep back out of the body into another world. This is a fine place for the mind to let go and explore if we don't dwell, doubt, stress, and attach to any one thought. Just lie back and observe your thoughts as if lying down watching the cloud roll by. *Savasana* is the king of yoga poses and should be done at the end each time you practice yoga. Here's how it's done:

1. Make sure you are warm enough. (Put on socks, clothing, or cover up with a blanket).
2. Lay completely flat on your back, palms up, arms and feet spread to a comfortable position. (Allow your feet to open out naturally)
3. Let your belly be soft to allow for natural breathing.
4. Let your bones be heavy and your skin soft like a corpse.
5. Let go completely...

CHAPTER 4

Mountain Pose & Sun Salutations

Rise up this mornin', Smiled with the risin' sun, Three little birds,
Pitch by my doorstep, Singin' sweet songs, Of melodies pure and true
Sayin', "This is my message to you,"Singin' "Don't worry about a thing, oh!,
Every little thing gonna be alright. Don't worry!"
Bob Marley

Mountain Pose is the first pose in Sun Salutations. Sun Salutations translate to "to bow or adore". Traditional yogis practiced these to deepen their connection to the world around them. They believed the sun represents our hearts and the moon our minds. Traditionally the sequence was 108 Sun Salutations practiced outdoors at sunrise, facing east. It was the yogis' ways of showing appreciation to Earth and all its' creatures. Remember, malas also have 108 beads on a string. There is a pattern with the number 108 in yoga.

Starting your morning with just a couple Sun Salutations can have the power to change how your entire day goes! A couple Sun Salutations are also great to prepare the body for meditation. From having the foundations of just Mountain Pose and Sun Salutations alone you will be able to create a basic yoga practice for yourself that you can do anytime, anywhere. Let's go over Mountain Pose...

Mountain pose is the foundation for every other pose. Most people will over look this pose, but to know and understand this pose is to understand all the rest. The pose starts from the ground up starting at your feet. It's like building a house. If the first layer of bricks is not solid, the house will have many problems and will not last long. Foundations are important in all parts of your lives. Taking the time to perfect your basics will save you time in the long run for everything. As a gymnasts you will definitely understand this!

In gymnastics we need to perfect our rolls, splits, and giants to have great flips, leaps, and Tkachev's. We can't be thrown in with the big dogs until we are properly trained as puppies. Without the basics in our practice, our gymnastics would be sloppy, and we would have more chance of getting injured. Without Mountain Pose our yoga poses would be empty. Mountain Pose is the anchor of the pose, just like our breath, that we can keep coming back to leading us on our way.

Mountain Pose aligns us so that we are standing properly in our bodies. Some people have been known to grow up to a couple inches taller just by standing correctly in their bodies. We slouch and hold our bodies in poor postures without even being aware of it. You will not only feel stronger and more alive in Mountain Pose, but you will stand prouder and feel more confident. Mountain Pose should be used when practicing yoga but also in everyday life. Keep your body aligned and your chakras and mind align more easily (chakras are energy bodies along the spine that we will touch base on later in the book).

It is important to know that all of the movements in Mountain Pose are very subtle. There are many subtleties in yoga. When you sit very still you can still feel subtle movements. Even in stillness there is much movement happening. Stop, feel, and notice those small subtle movements happening in and around your body while sitting still. Adjustments in the poses, especially in the beginning, do not need to be huge to create an impact. Perfect and well acquaint with Mountain Pose. The tedious work will pay off as you evolve in your practice.

Each pose, when learned correctly will have a story to tell you, and something new to teach you about yourself. Pay attention to each single detail of your body while in each pose. Pay attention to what part of the body the mind goes to. Pay attention to the breath. Pay attention to how you feel in the pose. This is key also. How you feel tells you a lot. Listen. Observe. Practice.

It is also very important to know how to stand correctly in your feet in order to build the perfect pose. There is an entire pose in just the feet! Study this diagram.

Use this diagram to help you understand the correct foot placement you should be using For yoga poses, gymnastics, and in general. You will become more sure footed and have better posture. The benefits will travel up!

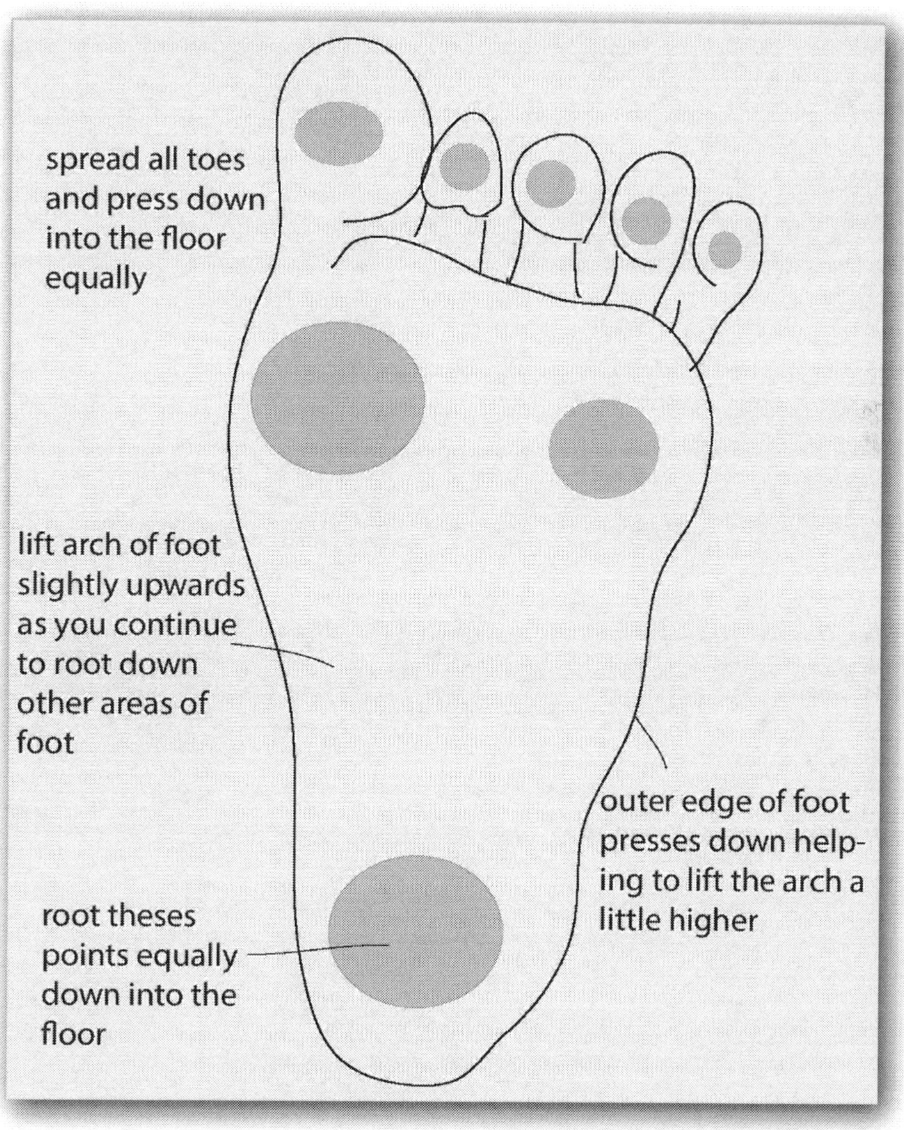

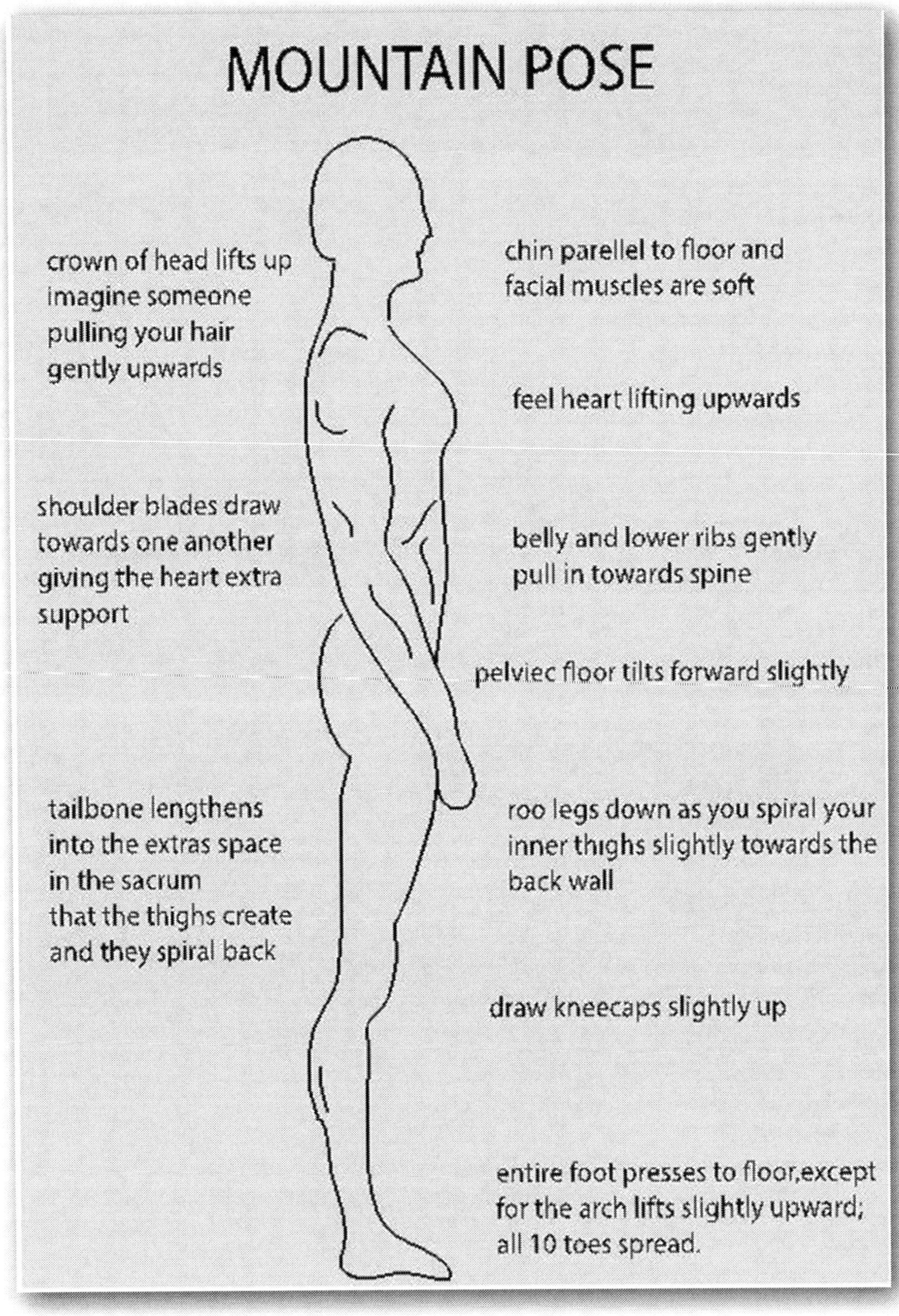

MOUNTAIN POSE

crown of head lifts up
imagine someone
pulling your hair
gently upwards

chin parellel to floor and
facial muscles are soft

feel heart lifting upwards

shoulder blades draw
towards one another
giving the heart extra
support

belly and lower ribs gently
pull in towards spine

pelviec floor tilts forward slightly

tailbone lengthens
into the extras space
in the sacrum
that the thighs create
and they spiral back

roo legs down as you spiral your
inner thighs slightly towards the
back wall

draw kneecaps slightly up

entire foot presses to floor,except
for the arch lifts slightly upward;
all 10 toes spread.

Let's take a moment and build* Mountain Pose *together, starting from your feet:

1. ***Feet are hip distance apart, or together, and rooting down***
2. ***Spread all 10 toes and press all parts of your feet down equally.***
3. ***Lift your leg muscles up, especially thighs, kneecaps lift lightly.***
4. ***Tilt the bottom of your pelvic floor gently forward drawing your belly in.***
5. ***Your lower ribcage pulls down integrating the core.***
6. ***Lift your heart slightly***
7. ***Shoulders back and down, palms forward, fingers long.***
8. ***Chin parallel to Earth, crown of your head pulling upward.***
9. ***Your gaze is steady. Mind, body, and breath are balanced.***

The 8 basic postures In Traditional Sun Salutations:

1. Mountain Pose (Tadasana)
2. Upward Salute (Urdhva Hastasana)
3. Forward Fold (Uttanasana)
4. Forward Fold ½ way up (Ardha Uttanasana)
5. Plank
6. Push-Up (Chatturanga)
7. Upward-Facing Dog (Urdhva Mukha Svanasana) or Cobra
8. Downward-Facing Dog (Adho Mukha Svanasana)

1. Begin in Mountain Pose.

2. Inhale and lift arms over head.

3. Exhale and fold forward.

4. Inhale ½ way up- torso parallel to Earth, gaze is straight down.

5. Exhale and step or hop back to plank.

6. Inhale and pause; exhale to Chatturanga- knees down or up.

7. Inhale to Upward Facing Dog (hands and tops of feet on floor only). or Cobra (entire belly remains on the floor and heart and knees lift).

8. Exhale into Downward Facing Dog.

CHAPTER 5

Yoga Poses

"An asana must be righteous and virtuous. By righteous I mean that it must be true. You must not cheat or pretend. You must fill every inch of your body with the asana from your chest and arms and legs to the tips of your fingers and toes, so that the asana radiates from the core of your body and fills the entire diameter and circumference of your limbs. You must Feel your intelligence, your awareness, and your consciousness in every part of your body."

-BKS IYENGAR

The Sanskrit name for a 'yoga pose' is asana. Asana is the 3rd Limb in the 8-Limb Path of Yoga, and it literally means "seat". In yoga, we want to feel strong yet relaxed in our poses. (*Sthira Sukham Asana*)We should also be striving for this same feeling in our gymnastics skill and routines. We should be striving this same feeling perhaps in our lives. See how yoga becomes a lifestyle?

This is what BKS Iyengar says about asana: "An asana must be righteous and virtuous. By righteous, I mean that it must be true. You must not cheat or pretend. You must fill every inch of your body with the asana from your chest and arms and legs to the tips of your fingers and toes, so that the asana radiates from the core of your body and fills the entire diameter and circumference of your limbs. You must feel your intelligence, your awareness, and your consciousness in every part of your body." It is the perfect description of what a pose becomes when we give it our all.

Asana works in the physical body in three ways: compressing, twisting, and stretching. Each pose is designed so that as our bodies are in each position the breath is lead into certain channels of our body that it wouldn't otherwise get to. This helps built-up toxins and tensions to be released. Fresh oxygen and prana are brought into areas that might have been dark and dusty. All of the bodies, the physical, mental, emotional, and spiritual layers, get touched on a deeper level. This is why we feel so relaxed, refreshed, and renewed after a yoga class. This is also why sometimes you may also feel emotional after a practice. You might touch into spaces that require your attention.

Muscular and Organic Energy

There are two kinds of energy, muscular and organic, that we work with while in asana. Muscular energy is when you are drawing energy in towards your center, and organic energy is when you are expanding energy out from your center. These opposing energies work together at the same time.

Muscular energy integrates the body and helps the pose to feel strong. You can think of it like you are hugging your skin to the bones and bones to the muscle, like 'shrink-wrap'. You energetically draw in towards your core as if your hands and feet had vacuums on them. Organic energy completes the full expression of the pose. As we draw our muscular energy in, at the same time, we lengthen and shine our limbs and entire body back out.

Yogis consider the spine the "tree of life". However old your spine feels is in direct relation to how old you will feel. Keep it healthy and flexible as you age! There are 33 individually stacked bones in the spine that connect all the way up to your brain. You can imagine your spine is like an antenna up to the Universe. From the base of the spine up to your brain should be aligned and healthy for optimal health. Yoga can help this!

The 5 parts of the spine are:

1. Cervical- neck
2. Thoracic- midback
3. Lumbar- lowback
4. Sacrum- between lumbar and tailbone
5. Coccyx Region- tailbone

The top 24 bones are moveable and the bottom 9 are fused together. The cervical spine has the greatest range of motion and is made up of 7 bones. The 12 bones of the thoracic spine vertebrae are connected to each rib and houses the heart and lungs. The lumbar spine is the largest part of the column and is between the ribcage and pelvis. The sacrum and coccyx are fused together and make up the pelvic girdle. All parts of the spine work together. Just as how our mind, body, and breath Trinity all need to be in sync, so do all parts of our spine. During each asana it is of utmost importance to pay attention to how our spines are aligned.

There are three stages to each asana- going in, holding, and coming out. We can think of it like a gymnastics routine- mounting, routine, and dismount. Each stage should go in and come out with control. The transitions between each asana should also go in and out of with the same control. You will know your yoga practice is evolving by the grace in your transitions. Try to make as least noise as possible, besides your breath, in your poses. This is a good indicator of a controlled practice.

Just as we wouldn't go right into our flips and skills without warming up, we want to warm-up the body, and mind, properly before going into asana, and meditation. (We warm-up for the poses with meditation. We warm up meditation with pranayama). Also, make sure your stomach is empty and that you're wearing comfortable clothing before practicing asana (and meditation). You won't want to wear socks for asanas since you will need full grip of your feet. Use your best judgment. If you're comfortable then the answer is *yes*

The following asana are listed in progression from "easy" to "harder". However, since all bodies are different, this may not be true for everyone. The poses with multiple photos next to the show progressions or modifications for the pose. We'll begin with standing poses, and then move into balancing, inversions, and backbends. Remember to have read and understand Chapter 2 & 3 completely before beginning asana so you can integrate the pose correctly with breath and Mountain Pose. Have fun and enjoy yourSELF!

STANDING ASANA
Standing poses usually begin a yoga class after your warm up poses. Standing poses work the entire body. They are good for learning balance, posture, and concentration. A class consist of a number of different standing poses. Mix them up to create a fun practice for yourself!
CHAIR POSE
EXTENDED SIDE
CRESCENT LUNGES VARIATIONS

CHAIR POSE (UTKATASANA)

Chair Pose helps to establish a firm foundation and stance for everyday living. It builds strength and muscles in the legs and increases balance, stability, and poise. Gaze will be straight forward or upward, depending on your neck strength and how it feels.

1. Start in Mountain Pose.
2. Keep your heart lifted upward as you sit back into an imaginary chair.
3. Arms will be straight up, palms facing one another.
4. Knees will be directly over your toes. If you look down you should be able to see your big toes, if not, just sit your hips back a little more.
5. Tailbone will draw downward and your lower ribcage pulls in toward your spine.
6. Find your Mountain, find your drishti, and find your breath. Hold for 3-10 breaths.

CRESCENT LUNGES (ANJANEYASANA) OR (ALASANA)

Crescent Lunges are a deep hip and thigh stretch for your back leg, whether your leg is up or down. The back leg is your anchor for the pose so keep is strong and grounded. This pose is great for strengthening your lower back and opening your upper back and shoulders.

1. Find the anchor in your back leg by feeling strong and supported in it. The back inner thigh should energetically spiral up towards the sky.
2. Draw your belly in slightly to help integrate your core.
3. Draw you lower ribcage in and subtly lift your heart.
4. Keep your shoulders plugging in and down as you lift your fingertips high, especially your pinkie fingers.
5. Find your Mountain, find your dristhi, and find your breath. Hold for 3-10 breath cycles.
6. Repeat on the other side.

EXTENDED SIDE ANGLE (UTTHITA PARSVAKONASANA)

Extended Side Angle Pose can be accessed through Warrior 2. Practicing this pose helps massage and stimulate your core organs and increase stamina. The pose also helps open the hips and release lower back suffocation. (Something most gymnasts have in common.)

1. Find your Mountain in Warrior 2.
2. Place your front hand on the ground to either side of your front foot (fingers tented or palm flat on ground). You can also place your elbow to knee for an easier modified version.

3. Extend your other arm straight up in the air, or reach it overhead in an angle, palm facing down.
4. Tuck chin slightly to keep back of your neck long.
5. Press down equally into both feet.
6. Find your Mountain, find your dristhi, and find your breath. Hold for 3-10 breath cycles.
7. Repeat on the other side.

WARRIOR 1
PRAYER TWIST
REVOLVED SIDE ANGLE

REVOLVED SIDE ANGLE (PARIVRTTA PARVAKONASANA)

Revolved Side Angle will be accessed through Warrior 1. The back foot can either be completely flat on the ground or the back heel can be up, knee facing ground. If the foot is flat the twist becomes more intense. This pose is great for revitalizing your organs and releasing toxins from the body and mind.

1. Start in Warrior 1.
2. Take the arm opposite your front foot and place your hand flat on the ground, or tent your fingers, to the outside of your foot.
3. Try to stack your shoulders and ribcage and keep your hips level to the floor. A slight twist in your pelvis is ok.
4. Extend your other arm straight up to the sky. Or, for more challenge, reach at an angle, so from the outer edge of your back foot you create a straight line out our fingertips. Palm faces down.
5. Find your Mountain, find your dristhi, and find your breath. Hold for 3-10 breath cycles.
6. Repeat on the other side.

PRAYER TWIST (PARIVRTTA UTKATASANA)

Prayer Twist begins in either Chair Pose or Crescent Lunge. From Chair Pose your feet and knees will come together and you will progress into the twist. (Your feet can be hip width apart, just make sure the feet are grounded and rooted before coming into the twist.) From Crescent Twist, your back knee can either be up or down. This pose is a twisting pose from the ribcage up. It helps to release toxins from your body as your organs are pressed together and massaged by the breath. The deeper you breathe the more toxins are released.

1. Start in Chair Pose or Crescent Lunge.
2. Bring your palms together in front of your heart and as you exhale start to come into our twist.
3. Bring your opposite elbow to your knee and your other elbow up towards the sky. Your fingers will face forward.
4. Stack your shoulders and ribcage as your press your palms together.
5. Keep your hips level to the floor. A slight twist in pelvic is ok.
6. Find your Mountain, find your dristhi, and find your breath. Hold for 3-10 breath cycles.
7. Repeat on the other side.

WARRIOR 1 (VIRABHADRASANA)

Warrior 1 is a powerful lunge. It helps to strengthen the knees, hips, legs, and more. The foot stance is if you were to draw an imaginary line from your front heel it should align with the arch of your back foot. This pose helps to improve your concentration, confidence, and coordination. Let's break it down...

1. Your front knee bends towards a 90-degree angle over your front foot.
2. Your back foot is at a 45-degree angle and the outer edge of your foot is firmly rooted into the ground. Pressing the outer edge of the foot down helps to engage the back leg and stabilize the pose. If the entire foot is not planted into the ground, step it forward until it is. If it is still too hard then stay with Crescent Lunge until your are able.
3. Square your hips the best you can towards the wall in front of you.
4. Relax your shoulders and square them evenly over your hips. Arms extend straight overhead, wrists over shoulders, palms facing each other, fingers spread, and pinkies lifting higher then rest of your fingers.
5. Find your Mountain, find your dristhi, and find your breath. Hold for 3-10 breath cycles.
6. Repeat on the other side.

WARRIOR 2
WARRIOR 3
TWISTING TRIANGLE
TRIANGLE

WARRIOR 2 (VIRABHADRASANA II)

Warrior 2 is a hip opener pose for the front leg. This pose helps to build concentration, strength, and focus. It also helps build strength and body awareness in the legs and arms. Warrior 2 can release tension in your lower back as well.

1. Start facing sideways on your mat, T your arms out to the side, palms down.
2. Step your legs apart so that each ankle comes directly under each wrist. This should be a good distance for your height.
3. Keep your toes, shoulders, and hips square to the wall as your turn your right toes towards the top of your mat. Your hips will want to turn also but keep them towards the wall by pressing your feet down and drawing muscular energy inward and upwards.
4. Bend your front knee so that it comes directly over your front ankle. Again, the hips will naturally want to move but keep them square as your press front knee out to your baby toe side.
5. Take your gaze over your front middle finger.
6. Find your Mountain, find your dristhi, and find your breath. Hold for 3-10 breath cycles.
7. Repeat on the other side.

WARRIOR 3 (VIRABHADRASANA III)

Warrior 3 is great for improving your focus, balance, and concentration. It improves core awareness and helps to calm the entire nervous system. You will build strength in your core, legs, and back muscles. You want to try to keep your body as straight as possible from your back heel, out your fingers, and perpendicular over your standing leg.

1. Stand in Mountain Pose.
2. Lift your arms overhead and interlace your fingers except for both pointer fingers will point straight up (like Charlie's Angels hands).
3. Slowly begin to lever forward as your back leg lifts up and you form the letter "T" with your body.
4. Keep lifted foot flexed and all 5 toes pointing towards the ground. This will helps keep your hips level.
5. Find your Mountain, find your dristhi, and find your breath. Hold for 3-10 breath cycles.
6. Repeat on the other side.

TRIANGLE POSE (UTTHITA TRIKONASANA)

Triangle Pose relieves stress and anxiety, alleviates back pain, and improves digestion. It helps build strength, balance, and coordination as well. Great for the core. This pose is also helpful to align the spine when done correctly.

1. Stand in a straddle with the arms out to a T, wrists aligned over your ankles, palms down.
2. Turn front toes all the way to the top of your mat and your back toes will be at a 45-degree angle.
3. Reach forward with your front hand as far forward as your can as you hinge your front hip under your back hip.
4. Keeping both side bodies as long as possible, keep the length in torso and drop the extended arm towards the ground or ankle (wherever it lands).
5. Stack your shoulders and extend the top arm straight up towards the sky with the palm facing outwards, fingers spread (imagine a light shining out your palm).
6. Find your Mountain, find your dristhi, and find your breath. Hold for 3-10 breath cycles.
7. Repeat on the other side.

TWISTING TRIANGLE (PARIVRITTA TRIKONASAN)

Twisting Triangle is another very deep twisting pose to help removes toxins from the body and mind. It is also great for increasing digestion, and relieving lower back pain. Triangle Pose increases coordination, balance, and focus.

1. Stand with your feet about 3 feet apart and your hips facing forward.
2. With your hands on your hips, bend forward so that your torso comes parallel to the ground. Keep pressing into both feet equally.
3. Place your opposite hand to the outside of your front foot, either flat or tenting the fingers.
4. Stack your shoulders and keep your hips level as you twist towards your front leg.
5. Extend your other arm straight overhead, palm open, fingers spread.
6. Find your Mountain, find your dristhi, and find your breath. Hold for 3-10 breath cycles.
7. Repeat on the other side.

PYRAMID VARIATIONS
HALF-MOON
TWISTING
HALF-MOON
MALASANA VARIATIONS

PYRAMID POSE (PARSVOTTANASANA)

Pyramid Pose stretches the hips and hamstrings, and lengthens the spine and neck. It helps to improve digestion and balance, and firms the legs. This pose is also great for calming the mind. You can use different arms positions depending on your shoulder flexibility. Try keeping hands on your hips, interlacing fingers behind you, reverse prayer, grabbing opposite elbow behind you, or keep arms straight overhead.

1. Start standing with your front foot about 2.5 feet in front of your back foot, hips and front toes forward, and back foot at 45-degrees..
2. Hands will be on your hips, or whoever best suits you (options above).
3. Bring your torso forward over your front leg.
4. Find your Mountain, find your dristhi, and find your breath. Hold for 3-10 breath cycles.
5. Repeat on the other side.

HALF-MOON POSE (ARDHA CHANDRASANA)

Half Moon Pose is great to help strengthen some of the smaller muscles in your ankles. A *must* for gymnasts, training athletes, tumblers, runners, and anyone who walks! It also strengthens the legs, core, and spine, and improves balance, coordination, and focus. Your top foot should be flexed, and toes spread, energetically press out your back heel as if standing on a wall behind. Arms are in prayer or open them straight up and down, palms out.

1. Start in Mountain Pose and lift your back leg as if going into Warrior 3. Instead of lifted toes pointing down though, open them out to a 90-degree angle in line with hips, shoulder and lifted knee.
2. Lower the same hand as your standing leg to the ground. Hand is flat on ground or fingers will tent.
3. Stack your shoulders and hips, and lift your top arm straight up to the sky. Palm opens outward and fingers spread. You can keep arms in prayer.
4. Find your Mountain, find your dristhi, and find your breath. Hold for 3-10 breath cycles.
5. Repeat on the other side.

TWISTING HALF MOON (PARIVRTTA ARDHA CHANDRASANA)

Let's access Twisting Triangle Pose from Warrior 3. Twisting Triangle is another very deep twisting pose which helps improve digestion, release toxins, and also relieves back pain. This pose is great for increasing balance, coordination, focus, and more.

1. Start in Warrior 3.
2. Place your opposite hand as your standing leg down on the ground directly under your shoulder. Take your opposite hand to your hip.

3. Once your feel grounded and stable, lift your hand that's at your hip up towards the sky and mindfully come into your twist.
4. Your gaze will be either to the ground, wall, or if your balanced take your gaze up towards the sky.
5. Find your Mountain, find your dristhi, and find your breath. Hold for 3-10 breath cycles.
6. Repeat on the other side.

GARLAND POSE (MALASANA)

Garland Pose is great for calming your nerves and revitalizing your organs and energy. If you ever feel nervous or anxious take this pose for instant relief. Combine with Forward Fold and Child's Pose for a rejuvenating mini practice. Garland Pose is great to aid in digestion or if you have cramps. It also helps relieve back pain. It is an overall feel good pose for mind, body, and soul!

1. Start in Mountain Pose, but with feet a little further then hip distance apart. Toes will turn our slightly.
2. Fold forward and bend at your knees so that your heels come off the ground. Place a folded or rolled blanket under your heels for added support if needed.
3. The middle of your spine will be directly over your heels, and your head and tailbone will bow equally forwards and backwards towards the Earth.
4. Tops of your arms will rest on the ground next to your feet, palms up, and fingers spread. Or bring your arms straight out to your sides, fingers tented and fingertips pressing into the floor. Keep your shoulders away from your ears.
5. Relax your face and neck.
6. Find your Mountain, find your dristhi, and find your breath. Hold for 3-10 breath cycles.
7. Repeat on the other side.

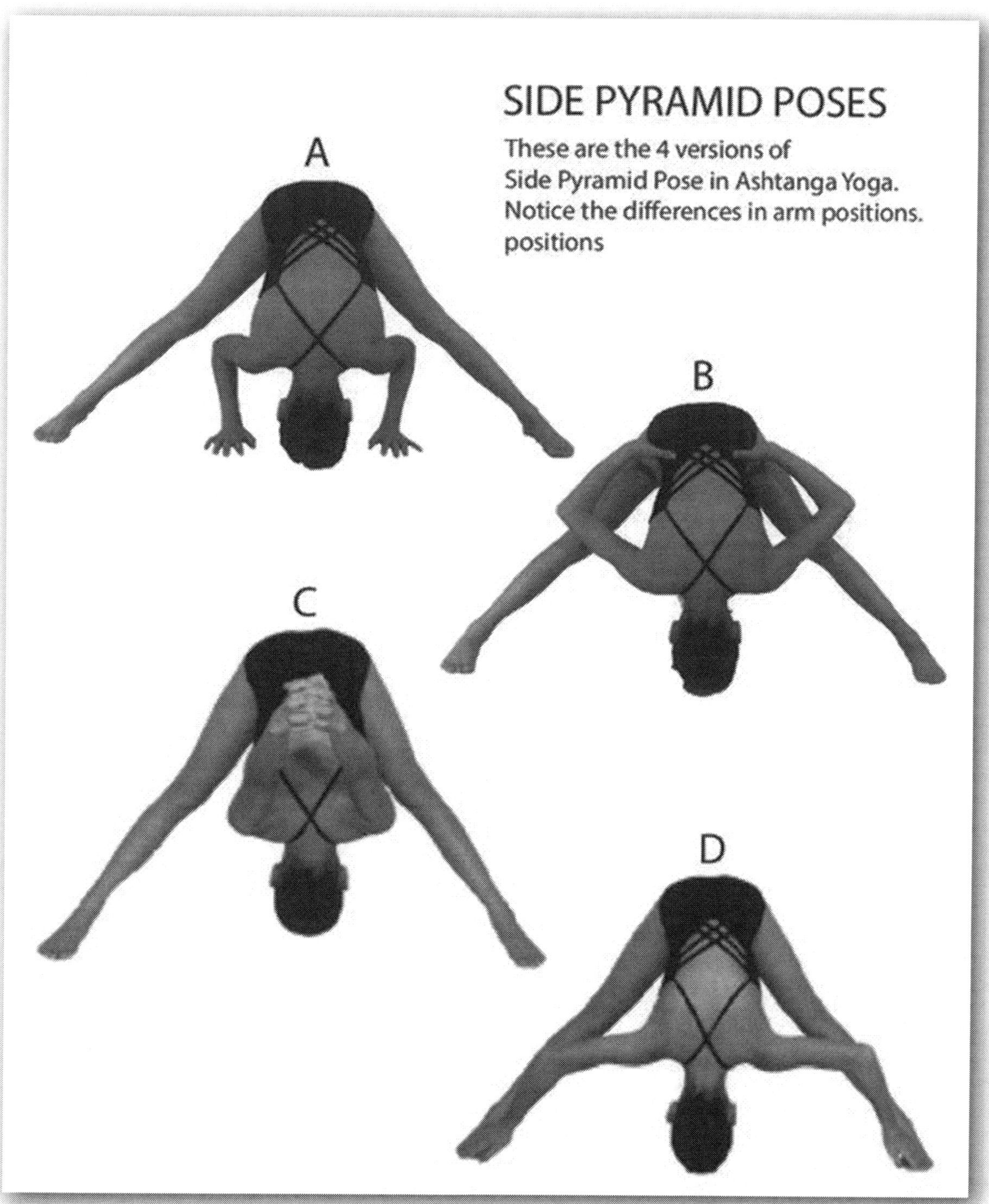
SIDE PYRAMID POSES
These are the 4 versions of
Side Pyramid Pose in Ashtanga Yoga.
Notice the differences in arm positions.
positions
A
B
C
D

SIDE PYRAMID POSE (PRASARITA PADOTTANASANA)

There are Side Pyramid A, B, C, and D in the Ashtanga Primary Series. We will cover all of them here for those who practice the Ashtanga versions of practice. Pyramids are inversions, (meaning upside down) that helps you to find balance, new perspectives, and balance in mind and body. These poses are great for strengthening your legs core, and more, creating overall body awareness.

A

1. Start standing in a straddle with your feet aligned under each wrist.
2. Inhale and lengthen spine as your bend forward until your torso is parallel to the ground, fingers tented on floor directly under your shoulders.
3. As you exhale, keep the length in your spine as you fold forward until the crown of your head comes to or towards to ground. Seat bones will lift high.
4. Your hands will come in line with your feet and press down into the floor keeping your elbows at a 90-degree angle and in line with your shoulders.
5. Find your Mountain, find your dristhi, and find your breath. Hold for 3-10 breath cycles.

B

1. Start standing in a straddle with your hands on your hips.
2. Inhale and look up, exhale and fold forward keeping side bodies and spine longs.
3. The crown of your head comes towards or gently on the ground.
4. Press strong into your legs and feet.
5. Stay soft in the facial muscles. Eyes should be slightly open.
6. Find your Mountain, find your dristhi, and find your breath. Hold for 3-10 breath cycles.

C

1. Start standing with your fingers interlaced behind your back, arms long and strong.
2. As you fold forward, bring your arms up and overhead.
3. Lift seat bones energetically upward as your lengthen crown of your head and spine to the ground.
4. Press strong into your legs and feet.
5. Stay soft in the facial muscles. Eyes should be slightly open.
6. Find your Mountain, find your dristhi, and find your breath. Hold for 3-10 breath cycles.

D

1. Start standing in a strong straddle mountain.
2. Fold forward and with your peace sign fingers of each hand grab your big toes of each foot.
3. Inhale as your find more length in your spine and reach side bodies out of your hips, and exhale come into the fold.
4. Keep your shoulders away from your ears and elbow up as your draw more length.
5. Press strong into your legs and feet.
6. Stay soft in the facial muscles. Eyes should be slightly open.
7. Find your Mountain, find your dristhi, and find your breath. Hold for 3-10 breath cycles.

CHANELLE STANDIFER IN
BALANCING POSES
Balancing Poses are good to help you find your center. It is very wise to practicing balancing poses daily. Start at a very young age and continue on for lifelong agility, focus, coordination, and strength. Balancing poses usually following standing poses in a yoga class.
STANDING HALF LOTUS
TOE HOLD
TOE STAND

TOE-STAND POSE (PADANGHUSTASANA)

Toe stand is another challenging pose. It helps to build strength in the standing ankle, foot, and leg. It also helps to improve focus, stabilization, and control in body and mind. This pose is also great for circulation and overall well being.

1. Start in Mountain Pose
2. Come up onto your toes and lower your seat slowly towards the ground as you ift the outer edge of one foot directly to the center of the opposite thigh. Your knee will be bent out to the side.
3. Place elbows on top of your knees and your palms placed together in front of your heart.
4. Balance on the standing toes. Use a block for support if needed with one hand to heart.
5. Find your Mountain, find your drishti, and find your breath for 3-10 breath cycles.
6. Repeat on the other side.

TOE-HOLD POSE (UTTHITA HAST PADANGUSTHASANA)

Toe-Hold is also in the Ashtanga Primary Series (which you will learn more about in Chapter 6). This pose helps you gain focus, strength, balance, and patience. You will also build the little muscles in the ankle and feet in this pose. Relieves tight hamstrings and lower back. The legs are also strengthened.

1. Stand in Mountain Pose.
2. Transfer your weight into one leg, bend the other knee up towards your chest and grab your big toe with your peace sign fingers. Your other hand will be placed on your hip.
3. Straighten your leg in front of you. Your foot is active and flexed as if standing on wall in front of you. Keep knee soft if needed to begin.
4. Find your Mountain, find your drishti, and find your breath for 3-10 breath cycles.
5. Repeat on the other side.

Standing HALF LOTUS (OPTION TO FOLD FORWARD) (ARDHA BADDHA PADMOTTANASANA)

Standing Half Lotus is also in the Ashtanga Primary Series. Stand holding foot with opposite hand, or reach around your lower back with the same arm and grab the top of your foot. If you have the bind (big toes or top of foot, or ankle) fold forward and place your free hand on the ground. This pose is great for improving balance, focus, coordination, and more.

1. Stand in Mountain Pose.
2. Bring outer edge of one foot into your opposite hip crease.
3. Place your palms together over your heart if your foot stays in place, or hold your foot with the opposite hand and keep other hand to your heart.
4. Find your Mountain, find your drishti, and find your breath for 3-10 breath cycles.
5. Repeat on the other side.

DANCER POSE
EAGLE POSE
TREE POSE

TREE POSE (VRKSASANA)

Tree Pose is one of the most classic yoga poses. To challenge yourself in this pose, if it isn't enough already, try closing your eyes, or gazing upwards. Notice the small bone movement in the ankles (subtle movement in stillness- this is a great pose in recognizing this concept.) You can even try to stand on your toes. Play around with different arm positions. Don't' forget, trees sway! So don't feel the need to be completely still.

1. Start in Mountain Pose.
2. Press down firmly into one leg as you lift the foot of the other leg into the inner thigh of the standing leg. Place your good either on the shin, ankle, or thigh. Never directly on the knee.
3. Place palms together over your heart and gather your balance and focus.
4. Take arms overhead as if your were a tree growing towards the sun.
5. Keep your spine straight and arms growing up as your shoulders stay relaxed down.
6. Find your Mountain, find your drishti, and find your breath for 3-10 breath cycles.
7. Repeat on the other side.

EAGLE POSE (GARUNDASANA)

Eagle Pose is a challenging pose that works your balance and focus. This pose strengthens and stretches your hips and shoulders. The positions your arms are in gets right into that hard to get spot in between your shoulders, the rhomboids.

1. Start in Mountain Pose.
2. Bend both knees slightly and as you press into one foot, the opposite leg will come up and around the standing leg.
3. With your arms straight out in front of you cross one arm on top of the other. Cross the opposite arm as the leg that's crossed over top. Bend your elbows as your try to spiral your palms (or backs of hands) together so they come in front of your face.
4. Find your Mountain, find your drishti, and find your breath for 3-10 breath cycles.
5. Repeat on the other side.

DANCER POSE (NATARAJASANA)

Dancer Pose is a graceful, yet strong, balancing yoga pose. It helps to open up and relieve and achy lower back, which many gymnasts are very used to! It is also great for opening up shoulders, and building focus, concentration, and body awareness.

1. Stand in Mountain Pose and spin one palm open to the side.

2. Keep knees together and bend one leg and catch it with same side hand.
3. Find your center and balance first, then begin to slowly press your foot into your hand as you lean forward and come into the pose.
4. Your torso will comes towards parallel to the ground.
5. Extend your free arm straight out in front of you as you align your wrist, shoulders, and hips.
6. Find your Mountain, find your drishti, and find your breath for 3-10 breath cycles.
7. Repeat on the other side.

EMERALD GORDON WULF IN BIRD OF PARADISE

BIRD OF PARADISE

Bird of Paradise yoga pose is probably the most challenging pose in this book. It is considered an advanced posture. Start feet at least hip distance apart in a forward fold with your knees bent. Reach one arm through your legs trying to get your shoulder behind the back of the same side knee. Reach as far as you can until the back of your hand reaches to your lower back, palm facing up. (Lift the same side heel to help wriggle hand up there.) Do not add on to this part until your hand is all the way comfortably up to your lower back. When it reaches there, move onto step 1. ...

1. Reach around your back with your other arm and when you can reach the wrist of your other hand move onto the next step.
2. Transfer all of your weight over to your free leg and root down to rise up slowly as your keep your eyes fixed to the ground.
3. Once you are all the way standing, you can try straightening your top leg.
4. Find your Mountain, find your drishti, and find your breath for 3-10 breath cycles.
5. Repeat on the other side

FLOOR ASANA

In a full yoga class, floor poses are typically practiced after standing and balancing poses. They usually are less vigorous and use less energy then standing poses. You can use them to cool down after a standing flow, or use a couple in the beginning to prepare your body for standing poses. Even in our floor poses, we engage with the subtle Mountain pose.

KATARINA DELCAMP IN LOTUS POSE

LOTUS POSE (PADMASANA)

Lotus Pose is another very classic yoga pose. It can be quite challenging, especially if you have sensitive ankle and knee joints. It helps to sit up on a folded blanket if you have tight hips. This pose helps to calm the body and mind. Be very patient with yourself in this pose, and as with all of the poses, never use any force.

1. Sit with your legs straight out in front of you.
2. Sit up tall with a strong upright spine and relaxed your shoulders down.
3. Bring the outer edge of one foot into your opposite hip crease. Try to relax your knees down. This is ½ Lotus. If this feels ok move onto the next step. Otherwise just work here in this pose.
4. Repeat step 3 with the other leg.
5. Find your Mountain, find your drishti, and find your breath. Hold for 3-10 breath cycles.

CHILDS POSE
RABBIT POSE
FORWARD FOLD
HEAD TO KNEE POSE

CHILD'S POSE

Child's Pose is a great restorative pose, also know as "thank God pose". Rest in it whenever needed. Take often This pose helps relieve indigestion and cramps, calms the nervous system, and quiets the mind. Come into Childs whenever you feel overwhelmed or anxious. It is very rejuvenating for the entire nervous system, even only after only a few short (I mean long, deep, steady) breaths.

1. Come onto your knees, toes together, knees apart or together.
2. Sit your seat bones onto your heels.
3. Bend your torso forward and place your forehead on the ground in front of you.
4. Arms can be either along your sides or overhead.
5. Take big, deep breaths into your back lungs.
6. Find your Mountain, find your drishti, and find your breath. Hold for 3-10 breath cycles.

RABBIT POSE

Rabbit Pose is one of the greatest overall poses you can do for body, mind, and soul. It is great for stimulating all of your organs, calming the mind, and opening along the entire back body. The thyroid gland is stimulated with the little bit of added pressure onto this area.

1. Start standing on your knees.
2. Begin to round your back and hunch your shoulders over so that the top of your head comes to the ground in front of you.
3. Reach your hands behind you and grab for your heels.
4. Lift your seat bones higher as you root your shins and knees down.
5. Find your Mountain, find your drishti, and find your breath. Hold for 3-10 breath cycles.

FORWARD FOLD (PASHIOMOTTANASANA)

Forward Folds are a common stretch for a gymnast. They are great for helping to elongate your spine and stretch your hamstrings. The difference in a yoga forward fold and a gymnastics forward fold is your heels will be flexed and your spine will be long, not round. This pose helps to relax your entire nervous system and stretches your entire back body

1. Start with your legs straight out in front of you, equal weight into both seat bones.
2. Flex both feet!
3. Keep your inner thighs energetically spiraling down towards the ground.
4. Inhale your arms overhead, and as you exhale keep your front body long as you fold over your legs.

5. Relax your face and neck.
6. Find your Mountain, find your drishti, and find your breath. Hold for 3-10 breath cycles.

HEAD TO KNEE POSE (JANU SIRSASANA)

Head to Knee Pose is a great yoga pose to help relieve stress in your body and mind. It is great for relieving pressure in the lower and upper back. It also opens the hamstring. Take this pose when you are feeling stressed or overwhelmed.

1. Start with your legs in front of you.
2. Bend one knee so that the bottom of the foot comes to the inside of your opposite thigh.
3. Keep your inner thigh spiraling down on your straight leg, and your torso long as you fold over your straight leg.
4. Keep your feet flexed and your spine pulling out from your hips as your relax your face.
5. Find your Mountain, find your drishti, and find your breath. Hold for 3-10 breath cycles.

THREAD THE NEEDLE
REVERSE TABLE
DIAMOND POSE

THREAD THE NEEDLE POSE

Thread the Needle Pose gets right into the juicy spot between the shoulder blades. This pose helps to relieve stress and will leave you feeling rejuvenated. It is a twist for the upper back. Be careful there is no pressure or weight in your neck.

1. Start on you hands and knees, shoulders over wrists, hips over knees.
2. Inhale as you lift one arm out to the side, and as you exhale "thread the needle" (sweep your arm under the other).
3. Place the arm through the opposite arm and leg. The entire top of arm, shoulder, and ear will come to the floor.
4. Keep your hips level to the floor and distribute weight equally into both knees.
5. Find your Mountain, find your drishti, and find your breath. Hold for 3-10 breath cycles.
6. Repeat on the other side

DIAMOND POSE

Diamond Pose is a deep hip opener pose and lower back reliever. It is good for the entire mind, body, and soul. Take often, especially when you are feeling tired or overwhelmed.

1. Sit on the ground with your seat bones rooting down, equally.
2. The bottoms of your feet come together. Keep your feet further out in front of you then you would for the classic *Butterfly Pose*. Your legs should form a diamond shape.
3. Place your forehead right into the inner arches of our feet. Your back can round here. Relax your face and neck.
4. To go deeper, take your arms inside of your legs and place your forearms under each calf.
5. To go even deeper, straighten your arms and spin the tops of them to the ground as they come behind you, hands will possibly touch.
6. Find your Mountain, find your drishti, and find your breath. Hold for 3-10 breath cycles.

REVERSE TABLE (PURVOTTANASANA)

Reverse Table Pose is just the opposite of Table Top, except your belly is facing up. This pose helps to open the entire front body, especially the shoulders, chest, and abdomen. It is great for circulation and building energy if you are feeling sluggish.

1. Sit on your seat with your knees bent and feet on the floor, hip width apart.
2. Place your hands behind you a comfortable distance, fingers face either towards you or directly behind you *whatever is most comfortable, or practice both).

3. Press your feet and hands into the ground as our bring your hips up creating a straight line from your shoulders to your knees.
4. Keep your gaze straight up, or if you have a strong neck, you can drop your head back.
5. Find your Mountain, find your drishti, and find your breath. Hold for 3-10 breath cycles.

BOAT POSE
FIRE LOGS
COW FACE POSE

BOAT POSE (NAVASANA)

Boat Pose is a great core developer which every single pose will benefit from a strong core. It helps improve strength, focus, and overall body conditioning.

1. Sit on the ground with your seat bones pressing equally down into the floor.
2. Bend your knees and place your feet on the floor. Support yourself under your thighs with our hands as you lean backwards to a 45-degree angle.
3. Lift your legs while keeping your spine aligned and lengthened at a 45-degree angle.
4. Keep knees bent to 90-degrees, or straighten them for more challenge.
5. Keep hands on your legs, or straighten your arms out to your sides, palms up.
6. Find your Mountain, find your drishti, and find your breath. Hold for 3-10 breath cycles.

COW FACE POSE (GOMUKHASANA)

Cow Face pose is a deep hip and shoulder opener for the notorious tight hips and shoulders of a gymnast. The arms are in an intense bind. Use a strap or sock if needed to help reach the hands if this is challenging for you at first. This pose helps to build concentration and focus.

1. Sit on the ground with legs out in front of you.
2. Cross your legs so that your knees are stacked, feet will be flexed to protect your knee and ankle joints.
3. Root your seat bones down. Use a blanket if your hips are really tight.
4. Reach one arm around your lower back and your other arm will come up and over head. Bend your elbows to bind the hands.
5. Find your Mountain, find your drishti, and find your breath. Hold for 3-10 breath cycles.

FIRE LOGS (AGNISTAMBHASANA)

Fire Logs Pose is another challenging hip and lower back opener, similar to Cow Face Pose. It helps to rejuvenate your entire body. Great hip opener. Agni in Sanskrit means "fire". You will feel the *fire* in this yoga pose in your hips.

1. Sit on the ground with your legs out in front of you.
2. Cross one leg over the other stacking your ankles and knees to form the shape of fire logs. Keep your feet flexed to protect your ankle and knee joints.
3. Sit up tall with a straight spine and relax your face and shoulders.
4. Hands can rest on your knees or bring into prayer in front of you heart.
5. Find your Mountain, find your drishti, and find your breath. Hold for 3-10 breath cycles.

SEATED TWIST
SPLITS
LIZARD POSE
PIGEON POSE

SEATED TWIST (MARICHYASANA C)

Practicing Seated Twist often will give you more freedom in your spine and neck. It also helps open your tight chest and shoulders. Seated Twist is great for digestion and detoxifying your organs.

1. Sit with your legs straight out in front of you in a pike position.
2. Bend one foot over you opposite leg so it comes to the outside of your knee.
3. Sit up tall and place the same hand as the bent knee directly behind you.
4. Inhale your opposite arm high in the air.
5. Exhale and twist bringing your opposite elbow to the outside of the bent knee. Gently look over your shoulder.
6. Keep shoulders back and down.
7. Find your Mountain, find your drishti, and find your breath. Hold for 3-10 breath cycles.

LIZARD POSE (UTTHAN PRISTHASANA)

Lizard Pose helps to release tight shoulders, hips, back, and neck. It also helps prepare the body for the more challenging pose, Pigeon Pose. Lizard will help rejuvenate your mind and body, while also helping to improve circulation.

1. Begin in a lunge.
2. Bring both hands to the inside of your front foot.
3. Bring your back knee and top of your back foot to the floor.
4. Bring both forearms down to the floor making sure you are not clenching in the body anywhere.
5. Find your Mountain, find your drishti, and find your breath. Hold for 3-10 breath cycles.
6. Repeat on the other side.

PIGEON POSE (EKA PADA RAJAKAPATASANA)

Pigeon Pose helps to open the forever tight gymnastics hips, and helps to open up the suffocation you may often feel in your lower back from tumbling and conditioning. It helps to rejuvanat the body while at the same time relax it through yoga practice. Pigeon is best accessed from Downward Dog. Take the modified version on your back if this is too intene. (Lie on your back and form the number 4 with your legs.)

1. Start in Downward Dog. Inhale and raise one leg up, exhale sweep that leg into Pigeon.
2. Your femur bone (large thigh muscle)will align with the side of your mat. Your knee will align just to the outside of your shoulder.

3. The back leg should extend long behind you, with an inner spiral of the leg, and knee and toes face the floor. Push downward with the baby toe to help level the hips to the ground.
4. Bring your forearms to the floor. If you are able, lay your entire torso and head down to the ground. Let go everywhere in mind and body, and get lost in our breath.
5. Find your Mountain, find your drishti, and find your breath. Hold for 3-10 breath cycles.
6. Repeat on the other side.

SPLITS (HANUMANASANA)

Splits are already going to be very familiar to you if you are a gymnast. The are probably the most common thing when it comes to gymnastics and yoga. Splits have endless benefits, just as every other pose. Follow your usual gymnastics splits techniques but notice the subtle differences here.

1. Come into your split but FLEX your front foot!
2. Find an inner spiral of the back inner thigh as you spin your pinkie toe down into the floor to help square your hips.
3. Lift up from the crown of your head creating length in your spine.
4. Palms come together in front of your heart or keep fingers gently to the ground along side of your body.
5. Find your Mountain, find your drishti, and find your breath. Hold for 3-10 breath cycles.
6. Repeat on the other side.

RECLINING TWIST
RECLINING
SCISSORS
INTENSE
THIGH
STRETCH
HAPPY BABY

RECLINING TWIST (SUPTA MATSYENDRASANA)

Reclining Twist is another great twisting pose for flushing toxins from your body and mind. This is similar to seated twist but a more restorative pose as the body lays comfortably on the ground. Take full advantage of the resting pose and take big deep breaths.

1. Lay flat on your back with arms and legs straight out, then draw one knee towards your chest.
2. Place your opposite hand to the outside of the knee as you come into the twist.
3. Your other arm will rest comfortable by your side.
4. Find your Mountain, find your drishti, and find your breath. Hold for 3-10 breath cycles.

RECLINING SCISSORS

Scissor Pose is a very intense twist but you can go as shallow or deep into it as feels good for you. Check in with yourself after each step to make sure you feel ready to go deeper. If not, back off and be patient. Just breate. Keep the bottom leg straight for less intensity.

1. Starting from Reclining Twist, straighten your bent knee and grab your foot or ankle with your opposite hand.
2. Bend your other leg and grab your foot or ankle with your free hand.
3. Find your Mountain, find your drishti, and find your breath. Hold for 3-10 breath cycles.
4. Repeat on the other side.

INTENSE THIGH STRETCH USING A WALL

This very intense thigh stretch is done with the support of the wall. Use blocks at first for extra support if you have very tight thighs. Start with your knee further from the wall. If you need more, inch it towards the wall. Be careful and listen closely to your body. Take your time getting into this pose.

1. Start in a lunge with the back knee bent and toes straight up the wall.
2. Slowly bring your hands to blocks outside of the front foot, or to your front knee.
3. When you are ready to go deeper, bring your hands down and scoot your back knee closer to the wall and reenter the pose.
4. Find your Mountain, find your drishti, and find your breath. Hold for 3-10 breath cycles.
5. Repeat on the other side.

HAPPY BABY POSE (ANANDA BALASANA)

Happy Baby Pose is such a great restorative pose and a great hip and lower back opener. Take this pose anytime of the day to relax and revive! If is for for both warming up and cooling down the body and mind. This pose is super for your overall well being.

1. Start lying down on your back, spine long and flat to floor.
2. Bend knees and flex feet upwards towards the sky.
3. Grab the outside edges of your feet with both hands and pull your knees down towards your armpits.
4. Find your Mountain, find your drishti, and find your breath. Hold for 3-10 breath cycles.
5. Repeat on the other side.

INVERSIONS

Inversions keep you young- from your skin, to your hair, to your mind. Think of them as a natural face-lift for the skin as you are reversing gravity upside-down!. They stimulate the brain, and give the heart a rest while the blood is drained to your vital organs. Plus, they give you a change of perspective. Do inversions anytime you feel sad, overwhelmed, or sad. They can help reverse negative effects. ⊠

WILD THING (CAMATKARASANA)

Wild Thing is another pose we can access from Downward Dog. It is a very organic pose, meaning alignment is not the key focus here. Rather, you feel into the pose and allow the body to open and express in its own way. This pose can help relieve your nervous system and opens your shoulders, hips, and mind.

1. Start from Downward Dog.
2. Inhale your right leg high and stack your right hip over your left hip as you actively press into your hands equally.
3. Hold this amazing stretch until you feel ready to "flip your dog".
4. Bring your right foot over and down to the ground.
5. Lift your right hand up towards the sky.
6. Explore moving the top arm in this pose and enjoy!
7. Hold for 3-10 breaths and repeat on the other side.

DOLPHIN POSE (ARDHA PINCHA MIYURASANA)

Dolphin Pose is similar to Downward Dog except your entire forearms are pressed to the ground. It is a great pose for opening your shoulders and chest. It builds strength in your arms and shoulders as well. Great beginning pose to work towards forearm stand.

1. Start in Downward Dog.
2. Slowly lower your forearms one at a time flat to the ground. Interlace your fingers around the back of your head.
3. Apply all of the principles from Downward Dog in Chapter 5 to this pose.
4. Find your Mountain, find your drishti and find your breath. Hold for 3-10 breath cycles.
5. Rest in Child's Pose for 3-10 breath cycles.

CROW POSE (BAKASANA)

Crow Pose is a vigorous arm-balancing pose. One of the first arm balancing poses learned in yoga is Crow. From Crow, you will build strength in your arms so you can learn more advanced arm balancing poses. This pose helps strengthen your wrists, chest, and arms. It also helps improve coordination. Just as standing poses build from the feet up, the pose on the hands build from the hands (since hands are touching the floor).

1. Start in Mountain Pose.
2. Bend your knees and place your hands on the ground directly in front of you, shoulder width apart, fingers forward.

3. Lock your arms and begin to lean your shoulders forward beyond your finger tips.
4. Lift and bend one knee at a time to your elbows as your engage the core and focus your eyes on your fingertips.
5. Find your Mountain, find your drishti and find your breath. Hold for 3-10 breath cycles.
6. Rest in Child's Pose for 3-10 breath cycles.

SHOULDER STAND (SALAMBA SARVANGASANA)

Shoulder Stand is known by many as the "Queen of Yoga Poses". It stimulates the entire nervous system. It puts pressure on our thyroid, which boosts your metabolism and gives you're an overall calming effect in your mind and body. Use a prop such as a folded blanket to take pressure off of your neck. The crease of the blanket will align with the top of your shoulders. Your head will hang off the blanket.

1. Start from Plow Pose.
2. Lift one leg at a time until your entire body is tacked on your shoulders.
3. Make sure no weight is in your neck. Come down and start again if you feel any pressure what so ever in your neck.
4. Root down into the backs of your arms to lift up taller through your toes.
5. Find your Mountain, find your drishti and find your breath. Hold for 3-10 breath cycles.
6. Rest in Child's Pose for 3-10 breath cycles.

HEADSTAND (SIRSASANA)

Headstand is know to many as the "King of Yoga Poses". The benefits are innumerable.

1. Start on your hands and knees.
2. Place your forearms on the ground like you do for Dolphin Pose and interlace all ten fingers behind your head.
3. Tuck your toes under and walk your feet forwards your face your so your hips begin to stack over your shoulders. Hold here or lift one leg up towards the sky.
4. If you feel steady and stable lift the other leg up.
5. Find your Mountain, find your drishti and find your breath. Hold for 3-10 breath cycles.
6. Rest in Child's Pose for 3-10 breath cycles.

HANDSTAND (ADHO MUKHA VRKASANA)

Handstands are a delicacy to a gymnasts. If you can rock a good handstand you will be likely to master many skills. A gymnastics handstand and a yogic handstand are slightly different. You will actually find your Mountain upside down starting with your hands. Use a wall for support if needed.

1. Start in Mountain Pose, arms overhead, lever into your handstand.
2. The hands are the foundation of the pose since they are touching the floor. Make sure the palms and fingers are strong.
3. Gently lift upward towards the sky and as someone tied string to your toes and are lifting you up.

4. Find your Mountain, find your drishti and find your breath. Hold for 3-10 breath cycles.
5. Rest in Child's Pose for 3-10 breath cycles.

PLOW POSE (HALASANA)

Plow Pose is a great yoga pose for the entire spine. Make sure there is no weight in your cervical spine (your neck). This is a great pose for your entire body and is recommended to do everyday. Use a prop, such as a folded blanket to help support your neck. The crease of the blanket will align with the top of your shoulders. Your head will hang off the blanket.

1. Start by laying flat on your back with your hips and shoulders evenly on the ground.
2. Pike your legs up overhead, supporting your lower back with your heads as you do so.
3. Your toes will come onto the ground over your head, and after they do, spiral your shoulders under more and lift chin slightly off your chest.
4. Find your Mountain, find your drishti and find your breath. Hold for 3-10 breath cycles.
5. Rest in Child's Pose for 3-10 breath cycles.

FISH POSE (MATSYASANA)

Fish Pose is a counter pose for both Shoulder Stand and Headstand. It helps to open up the entire central channel of the body and mind. Add Lion's Breath to this pose for added stimulation.

1. Lay flat on your back.
2. Tuck arms close to your sides so that your thumbs and index fingers comes just under your body.
3. Press down into your forearms and hands, and puff your chest and chin up towards the sky.
4. Place the top of your head to the ground, throat up to the sky.
5. Find your Mountain, find your drishti and find your breath. Hold for 3-10 breath cycles. (Option for Lion's Breath)

BACKBENDS

Backbends are invigorating, no matter the size or modification. Even looking up towards the sky can be the beginning of a backbend. Backbends are great to do when you are feeling down, depressed, or if you are a woman on your moon cycle. Looking up towards the sky is the beginning of a very simple backbend. In fact, as much a we look at our phones each day, look up to the sky often to counter pose this action. Enjoy a backbend every-day!

CAMEL POSE (USTRASANA)

Camel Pose invigorates the entire body. It opens your heart and lungs, and makes you feel rejuvenated. Do the pose with both hands back grabbing each heel at the same time, or for a simpler version, grab one heel at a time and raise free arm towards the sky

1. Stand on your knees, hip width apart.
2. Turn your toes under for more support, like kickstands, or keep tops of the feet flat on the ground.
3. Bring right hand first to your right heel. If everything feels ok, bring your other hand to the other heel.
4. Integrate your core by pulling the lower ribs back towards your spine. Lift into the backbend from your heart and gaze.
5. Only if your neck feels good you can drop your head all the way back, otherwise keep your gaze forward, or to the sky.
6. Find your Mountain, find your drishti, and find your breath for 3-10 breath cycles.
7. Rest in Child's Pose for 3-10 breath cycles.

BRIDGE POSE (SETU BANDHA SARVANGASANA)

Bridge Pose is another pose that stimulates the thyroid gland. It is invigorating and not quite as intense as Plow or Shoulder Stand. This pose is great for overall mind, body, and soul, and helps to relax your brain.

1. Start lying on the floor with your knees bent, and feet flat on the ground hip-width apart.
2. Arms are straight down by your sides, palms down.
3. Press down into your feet and arms. As you roll your body up, starting from your tailbone, feel each vertebrae lift from the ground.
4. Tuck your shoulders under you more if you can and interlace your fingers underneath you.
5. Lift your chin slightly to allow proper air flow.
6. Find your Mountain, find your drishti, and find your breath for 3-10 breath cycles.

FULL WHEEL (URDHVA DHANURASANA)

Full Wheel is another yoga pose that is just like a gymnastics skill. A full wheel is basically a backbend that you're used to in gymnastics. The entire front body is stretched and toned. This pose is great for when you feel sluggish or sad. A backbend can brighten your day. A backbend a day helps keep the blues away!

1. Start lying on your back.
2. Bend your knees and bring your feet flat to the ground while rooting all four corners of your feet down.

3. Bend your arms so that your hands are flat on the ground right over your shoulders, fingers facing you, and elbows high aligning over your shoulders.
4. Press down into your hands and feet equally as you lift our belly upwards to the sky. Keep core integrated.
5. Find your Mountain, find your drishti, and find your breath for 3-10 breath cycles.
6. Rest on your back (or in Child's Pose) for 3-10 breath cycles.

BOW POSE (DHANURASANA)

Bow Pose is a Full Wheel flipped upside-down, on your belly. You will rock slightly with your breath, and this creates an amazing massage for the abdomen. All of the organs are stimulated and this is great for digestion and releasing toxins in the organs. Bow Pose calms your entire nervous system, and opens your chest, lungs, and heart.

1. Lay flat on your belly with your arms by your sides.
2. Bend your knees, flex your feet, and reach for both ankles with your hands.
3. Integrate your core as your come into your backbend. Lift your chest and gaze.
4. Allow the body to rock as you breathe. You can choose to rock slightly or bigger.
5. Find your Mountain, find your drishti, and find your breath for 3-10 breath cycles.
6. Rest flat on your belly for 3-10 breath cycles.

These are a just a small number of yoga poses that exist in the world today. There are many more, but this will be a great starting point for you. Practice these poses daily, even if only for 5 minutes. You will notice an enormous increase in your physical, mental, and emotional health. Share your poses on Instagram at @yogaforgymnasts and follow my page for tutorials and more inspiration. Message me and let me know you are doing. I'd love to keep in touch!

In the next chapter we will go over how to build your own special practice. We are all different, so don't get caught up in having a "perfect" practice or one that looks like someone else's. Remember, your style may change during certain seasons or times of your life too. As long as you are incorporating the mountain, the breath, and the dristhti into your practice then you are on the right track. It does not matter how far you go into a pose. If you have the mountain, the drishti and the breath in sync you are reaping all the benefits. You will also notice with practice how far you will be able to go in time. Don't give up. and have fun. Let's build your very own customized yoga practice now.

CHAPTER 6

Creating Your Very Own Yoga Practice

"The world is but a canvas to our imaginations"
Henry David Thoreau

Hopefully by now, you have a better understanding of yoga, and have practiced at least a few of the asana from this book. In this chapter, you will be able to incorporate what you've learned so far and create a practice for yourself, which you can enjoy in the convenience of your own home.

Want to make learning a practice or sequence really easy on yourself? Practice Sun Salutations everyday for one month doing 3-5 rounds. Just learning and practicing these will teach you a lot and you will be inspired to add on more sequences and styles from there. Let's customize a yoga practice that feels good to YOU, in your amazingly unique body.

Simple Yoga Practice

A simple formula to design a home practice: Meditate + asana+ savasana

1. Meditate- primes you for the poses. It helps to clear mental space so you are more present to what your body is doing. Sit for 1-10 minutes.
2. Asana- will consist anywhere from 1-30 poses, depending on the amount of time you have and your energy level for that day.

3. Savasana- can be held anywhere from 1-20 minutes. The body is very intelligent so we learn in this pose to let go and the let body works its magic!

Energizing Yoga Practice

We can easily add on to the above formula to create a much longer practice. You will start in meditation, then add 1-3 Sun Salutations, plus 1-3 poses from each category: standing, balancing, floor poses, inversions, and backbends. Then finish with Savasana.

Here's an example of an extended version of the simple yoga practice:

1. Seated Meditation
2. Sun Salutations
3. Warrior 2
4. Reverse Warrior
5. Tree Pose
6. Natarajasana
7. Marichyasana A
8. Marichyasana B
9. Shoulderstand
10. Bridge
11. Wheel
12. Savasana

Find a comfortable seated position and breathe for 1-10 minutes. Feel stable and grounded in your Mountain as you begin your rounds of Sun Salutations. Then, move into Warrior 2 and Reverse Warrior on each side. You can do both on each side before switching sides. Finish the rest of the poses in order and then come into final Savasana for 3-10 minutes.

Congratulations! You have just completed a yoga practice. Great job! ☺ This specific practice should take you anywhere from 15-30 minutes; depending on how long you hold each pose.

Plan beforehand which poses you will practice. You can even write them down and tape the sequence to a wall in front of where you are practicing. This way you can get more into your practice rather then flipping through the pages and breaking your flow.

Start in Mountain Pose. Feel stable and strong as you begin to move into your first Sun Salutations. Practice a few rounds of Sun Salutations before coming into the remainder of the asana.

You now have many simple options to start your own yoga practice:

1. Just Meditation
2. Just Sun Salutations

3. Just single Asanas
4. Combine Meditation, Sun Salutations, and Asanas

Here are some more...

Vinyasa Yoga Practice

To take it even one step further, we can add Vinyasa between each asana, either after each side, or after each round. Make the practice more or less challenging by varying the number of poses in each sequence as well as the length of times in each pose.

Vinyasa means, "to flow". It is simply a way to connect poses so that the practice becomes more fluid and dance-like. Vinyasa can be healing on the body and mind, and added anywhere in your practice to help recharge you. Vinyasa is great for gymnasts because it can provide great conditioning without wear and tear on your body.

Here is an example of a Vinyasa Yoga class:

1. Seated Meditation
2. Sun Salutations
3. From Downdog, inhale your right leg high, exhale and step it through to right hand. Inhale into first asana of your sequence (example: inhale to Crescent).
4. After your 2-3 poses on that side, take a Vinyasa.
5. Repeat on other side- inhale left leg high, exhale step it through to left hand, and inhale into same sequence you did on the right side.
6. "Take a Vinyasa"
7. From Downward Dog, step or hop to top of mat, inhale half way up, and exhale fold.
8. Inhale come all the way up and exhale hands to your heart.
9. Begin your next sequence.
10. Finish the rest of the poses in order and then come into final Savasana for 3-10 minutes.

Find a comfortable seated position and breathe for 1-10 minutes. Feel stable and grounded in your Mountain as you begin your rounds of Sun Salutations. Then, move into your first sequence of poses. After your two sequences you will do 1-2 balancing poses. From balancing poses you will do one inversion, 2-3 floor poses, and 1-2 backbends. End in a 3-10 minute Savasana.

As your practice evolves, play around with harder poses, and get creative. Breathe 2-5 cycles in each asana, on each side. Eventually you might try to move so that each movement is only one big, deep, steady, breath. The goal is to have the least amount of fidgeting or movement happening between your transitions. Do your best not to loose track of the controlled breath during transitions. The more we learn to control our breath in the asana practice, the more we are able to control our minds and body in life; they are all connected.

Here are two more examples of classes you could practice. They are from the Ashtanga lineage. Ashtanga is one of the most traditional styles of yoga, and is excellent for gymnasts since so much emphasis is on alignment. Ashtanga is meant to be practiced the same way, everyday, and is made up of six series. We will learn here about the first series. Lets break it down into two different practices: a modified version of the first series, and then a modified version of the Primary Series.

Modified Ashtanga First Series

Here is an example of a modified first series class:

1. Seated Meditation
2. Sun Salutations
3. Triangle
4. Reverse Triangle
5. Extended Side Angle Pose
6. Revolved Side Angle Pose
7. Side Pyramid A, B, C, D
8. Front Pyramid
9. Toe Hold
10. Half Lotus Fold
11. Chair Pose
12. Vinyasa
13. Warrior 1
14. Warrior 2
15. Vinyasa
16. Savasana

Find a comfortable seated position and breathe for 1-10 minutes. Feel stable and grounded in your Mountain as you begin your rounds of Sun Salutations.

From Mountain Pose, step your right foot about 3 feet back, and turn so that you are facing the back of your mat in Triangle Pose feet. Mindfully move into Triangle and hold for 3-5 seconds. Come up out of the pose and turn feet to face the front of your mat to take triangle pose on your left side. Hold 3-5 seconds. Come up out of the pose, and step together to Mountain Pose at the top of your mat.

From Mountain Pose, step your right foot about 3 feet back, and turn around to do Reverse Triangle Pose facing the back of your mat, on your right side. Hold 3-5 seconds. Come up out of the pose and turn feet to face the front of your mat to take Reverse Triangle Pose on your left side. Hold 3-5 seconds. Come up out of the pose, and step together to Mountain Pose at the top of your mat.

From Mountain Pose, step your right foot about 3 feet back, and turn around to do Extended Side Angle Pose facing the back of your mat, on your right side. Hold 3-5 seconds. Come up out of the pose and turn feet to face the front of your mat to take Extended Side Angle Pose on your left side. Hold 3-5 seconds. Come up out of the pose, and step together to Mountain Pose at the top of your mat.

From Mountain Pose, step your right foot about 3 feet back, and turn around to do Revolved Side Angle Pose facing the back of your mat, on your right side. Hold 3-5 seconds. Come up out of the pose and turn feet to face the front of your mat to take Revolved Side Angle Pose on your left side. Hold 3-5 seconds. Come up out of the pose, and step together to Mountain Pose at the top of your mat.

From Mountain Pose, step feet wide apart so you are facing sideways on your mat. With your arms out to a T, feet aligned under your wrists. Inhale, look up and elongate the spine, exhale fold into Side Pyramid A, B, C, and D. Hold each for 3-5 seconds. Inhale as you come up between each one; exhale as you fold into each one. After Side Pyramid D, step your feet together at the top of your yoga mat.

From Mountain Pose, step back right foot about two and a half feet, and turn entire body to face the back of your mat. Inhale look up, exhale fold into Front Pyramid. Hold for 3-5 seconds. Come up out of the pose and turn to the front of your mat for your left side Front Pyramid. Hold 3-5 seconds. Come up out of the pose, and step together to Mountain Pose at the top of your mat.

From Mountain Pose, start with your right leg for Toe Hold, and then move to your left side. Hold 3-5 seconds each side. Then go into Half Lotus Fold on each side, starting with your right foot, and hold for 3-5 seconds. Come into Chair Pose and hold for 5-10 seconds. From Chair Pose, exhale and fold into your Vinyasa.

From Downward Dog, step your right foot to your right hand and come up into Warrior 1. Hold 3-5 seconds. Pivot your feet by turning the right foot in and the left foot out. Bend the left knee, and hold Warrior 1 on the left side for 3-5 seconds.

Exhale into Warrior 2 on your left side, facing the back of your yoga mat. Hold 3-5 seconds. Straighten your left leg and pivot your toes to take Warrior 2 facing the front of your mat. Hold for 3-5 breaths. Cartwheel your arms down to take your last Vinyasa. Hold Downward Dog for 3- 5 breaths before moving into final Savasana.

Modified Ashtanga Primary Series

Here is an example of modified primary series class:

1. Seated Meditation
2. Cat/Cow
3. Sun Salutations
4. Triangle
5. Reverse Triangle
6. Extended Side Angle Pose
7. Revolved Side Angle Pose
8. Side Pyramid A, B, C, D
9. Front Pyramid
10. Toe Hold
11. Half Lotus Fold
12. Chair Pose
13. Vinyasa
14. Warrior 1
15. Warrior 2
16. Vinyasa
17. Seated Forward Fold
18. Vinyasa
19. Reverse Table
20. Vinyasa
21. Head to Knee Pose
22. Vinyasa
23. Seated Twist
24. Vinyasa
25. Bow Pose
26. Vinyasa
27. Seated Angle Pose
28. Vinyasa
29. Shoulder Stand
30. Fish Pose
31. Savasana

Find a comfortable seated position. Set your timer for 5 minutes. Sit still in meditation. Watch your mind run at first, then use your breath. Inhale and count to four. As you exhale count to four. The breath will help slowly dissipate the mind, creating a more clear slate for your practice to be present and experienced. After the timer goes off, open your eyes slowly.

Do a couple rounds of Cat/Cow. Start on all fours in tabletop position, inhale as you lift the heart and gaze, exhale as you round through the spine. Stand up and find your Mountain Pose. Feel stable and strong as you begin to move into your first Sun Salutations. Practice a few rounds of Sun Salutations A and B, before continuing on with your standing asanas.

From Mountain Pose, step your right foot about 3 feet back, and turn around to do Triangle Pose facing the back of your mat, on your right side. Hold for 3-5 seconds. Come up out of the pose and turn feet to face the front of your mat to take triangle pose on your left side. Hold 3-5 seconds. Come up out of the pose, and step together to Mountain Pose at the top of your mat.

From Mountain Pose, step your right foot about 3 feet back, and turn around to do Reverse Triangle Pose facing the back of your mat, on your right side. Hold 3-5 seconds. Come up out of the pose and turn feet to face the front of your mat to take Reverse Triangle Pose on your left side. Hold 3-5 seconds. Come up out of the pose, and step together to Mountain Pose at the top of your mat.

From Mountain Pose, step your right foot about 3 feet back, and turn around to do Extended Side Angle Pose facing the back of your mat, on your right side. Hold 3-5 seconds. Come up out of the pose and turn feet to face the front of your mat to take Extended Side Angle Pose on your left side. Hold 3-5 seconds. Come up out of the pose, and step together to Mountain Pose at the top of your mat.

From Mountain Pose, step your right foot about 3 feet back, and turn around to do Revolved Side Angle Pose facing the back of your mat, on your right side. Hold 3-5 seconds. Come up out of the pose and turn feet to face the front of your mat to take Revolved Side Angle Pose on your left side. Hold 3-5 seconds. Come up out of the pose, and step together to Mountain Pose at the top of your mat.

From Mountain Pose, step feet wide apart so you are facing sideways on your mat. With your arms out to a T, feet aligned under your wrists. Inhale, look up and elongate the spine, exhale fold into Side Pyramid A, B, C, and D. Hold each for 3-5 seconds. Inhale as you come up between each one; exhale as you fold into each one. After Side Pyramid D, step your feet together at the top of your yoga mat.

From Mountain Pose, step back right foot about two and a half feet, and turn entire body to face the back of your mat. Inhale look up, exhale fold into Front Pyramid. Hold for 3-5 seconds. Come up out of the pose and turn to the front of your mat for your left side Front Pyramid. Hold 3-5 seconds. Come up out of the pose, and step together to Mountain Pose at the top of your mat.

From Mountain Pose, start with your right leg for Toe Hold, and then move to your left side. Hold 3-5 seconds each side. Then go into Half Lotus Fold on each side, starting with your right foot, and hold for 3-5 seconds. Come into Chair Pose and hold for 5-10 seconds.

From Chair Pose, exhale and fold into your Vinyasa.

From Downward Dog, step your right foot to your right hand and come up into Warrior 1. Hold 3-5 seconds. Pivot your feet by turning the right foot in and the left foot out. Bend the left knee, and hold Warrior 1 on the left side for 3-5 seconds.

Exhale into Warrior 2 on your left side, facing the back of your yoga mat. Hold 3-5 seconds. Straighten your left leg and pivot your toes to take Warrior 2 facing the front of your mat. Hold for 3-5 breaths. Cartwheel your arms down to take your Vinyasa. From Downward Dog, jump or walk through to a seat with your legs straight out in front of you.

Inhale and lengthen your spine, exhale and fold into your Seated Forward Fold. Hold 3-5 seconds. Take a Vinyasa. Come into Reverse Table for 3-5 seconds, and then take a Vinyasa. Start with your right leg Head to Knee Pose, hold 3-5 seconds, and then repeat on your left side. Take a Vinyasa, and then come to Seated Twist, starting with your right side, holding for 3-5 seconds.

From Seated Twist on your left side, take a Vinyasa, and then come into Bow Pose. Hold Bow Pose for up to 30 seconds, and then take a Vinyasa. Remember, some of these Vinyasas can be omitted if you are losing control of your breath, or if you are feeling winded. It is unlikely at first that you will do all of them, so use your best judgment to where you might leave some out until you build the strength.

From Downward Dog, start with Seated Angle Pose on your right side, hold for 3-5 seconds, then switch to your left side. Take your Vinyasa. Come into Shoulder Stand for up to 5 minutes, and counter pose with Fish Pose for 5 round of breaths. Prepare for final Savasana. Put on socks and long sleeves if desired, and stay in Savasana for up to 30 minutes. Let the practice absorb into your body as you lay down and indulge in this peaceful energy soak.

Now you have all the information you need to create your very own custom yoga practice. Another practice you could try when you are feeling creative or inspired is just put the music on to something mellow, or to some of your favorite hip-hop beats and "free flow". It feels good to go completely out of the box, let your mind go, and allow the body to move without any sort of plan or agenda. Let your body organically move into the places and spaces that are feeling tight, or that just need your special attention as you come into them. Make sure as you practice you incorporate a breath pattern as you move- inhaling as the body expands; exhaling as the body contracts; Inhaling as the body lifts, exhaling as the body lowers. Make it dance-like, make it honest, and stay present. You might even be slightly surprised with other new yoga poses that just happen in your body. Have fun, stay calm, and breathe.

Another way to further learn about yoga sequencing is to watch YouTube, rent dvd's, subscribe to an online channel, get friends together to practice, or go to yoga classes. All of these ways will inspire more ideas and teach you more about the yoga practice. As with anything, the more we study and practice, the better we become at it, and yoga knowledge is readily available today. We are at a blessed time here in the West to have this practice available to us in such an accessible way. So get out your magic carpets and fly!

CHAPTER 7

Yoga for Recovery

"Sometimes the road forward seems backwards..."
RUMI

As a competitive gymnast I remember always having some sort of bump, bruise, or injury at any given point. Whether it was a serious injury, such a fracturing both my ankles at the same time while tumbling- I fractured one foot coming out of my back handspring and fractured the other coming out of my full. My body was on autopilot, as it was so used to always being on, and so I continued to still go for the entire tumbling pass even after the first break! Then there was the knee surgery after hyper extending my knee while front tumbling, stepping out of my front tuck, and jarring me knee so far back I collapsed to the floor in tears. Oh yeah! The time I would've broke my neck if my coach Fig wouldn't have caught me by my T-shirt after hitting my head on the back flyaway off the high bar. I held on too long to the bar and the back of my head banged the bar at full speed landing me unconscious to the ground with two huge bruised cheeks and unappealing black eyes. The stitches to the head when I split my skull open on the balance beam doing my double back handspring, double twist dismount was one of the worst. I didn't feel anything at first, but when I woke up from being knocked unconscious once again, I had a handful of blood. That's when the tears started rolling. I remember the huge needles they injected into my head at the hospital that night before sewing my head back together. I think that was more terrifying then the fall!

With all this said, you can see how incredibly tough the sport of gymnastics is on the body. These were not even that serious. Gymnasts are some of the toughest athletes in the world. Yoga is a good counter practice to the impact from the drilling, pounding, tumbling, and repetitions in gymnastics. The benefits your body and mind receive from practicing yoga make it so you have a less chance of even getting injured in the first place. Now it's not to say yoga prevents injury, accidents happen, but you will become more mindful, meaning fewer mistakes, and if you do become injured, recovery can happen faster.

If you are out of gymnastics practice due to an injury, do not fret. Yoga is the perfect gateway to save the day. Or, should I say, to save the body! You can use the poses in this chapter if you can't participate in your regular gymnastics practice while you're recovering. You can also practice these poses if you are sore from practice and want to cool down. The support from the props make it so your body gets a great stretch while fully relaxed in body and mind.

Most of the poses and practices in this book can be modified if you have an injury by using good judgment, and props (bolsters, blankets, blocks, and straps.) In this chapter though, we will go over some available Restorative Poses that you can explore. If you are coming back from an injury and starting out slowly, start with this chapter. If you have a more serious injury such as a broken ankle or knee surgery, practice single poses with no flow. If you are a little longer into your recovery, you may be able to add flow to some of the poses. Just use your best judgment. Your body will talk to you. Listen carefully! Allow the feelings, sensations, and breaths in your body to be your best guide to help determine which poses will be best for you during this sensitive time. You don't want to over exert or add strain while in recovery.

The point of yoga is to restore the body, not break it down. Yoga for recovery consists of easy poses that are held longer. Holding poses for longer than a minute allows the body to restore and heal itself physically, mentally, and energetically. The skeleton and connective tissue have time to rebuild. We have more time for the breath. Through yoga for recovery we learn to transform stagnant energy from our injury into potential energy.

Some of the most common injuries for gymnasts are:

1. **Sprained Wrists-** The wrists are the most used body part of the gymnast. They are used for tumbling on floor and beam, for vaulting, and for uneven bars. The ligaments get easily overworked, stretched, torn, and strained. Yoga poses help to build stronger hands, fingers, and wrists. The wrist joints also become more fluid.
2. **Sprained Ankles-** the ankles are also very heavily used for gymnasts. Most commonly, sprained ankles occur from falling and landing short, or rolling the ankles while tumbling or dismounting. Yoga poses help to strengthen the ankles. Also, just learning to stand on your foot correctly, as discussed in Chapter 4, can prevent injury from happening.
3. **Knee Sprain or Tears-** Knee sprains or tears most often occur from hyper extending, twisting, or under landing on a skill or dismount. Yoga poses teach you to align your body correctly which puts less strain on the knees and helps prevent injury.
4. **Achillie Tendonitis-** The achillie is above the back of the heel. It gets pulled easily in tumbling or landings, especially when under landing, or from overuse. This creates pain all of the way up the calve. Yoga helps to strengthen small bones and muscles around the ankle helping to prevent this injury.
5. **Upper Back and Shoulder Strain-** Injury or pain can occur in the upper back and shoulders from the pressure, weight, and impact of gymnastics practice. The swinging, pushing,

pressing, and blocking strains the shoulders and back. Yoga helps to lubricate the joints and strengthens the shoulders.

6. **Mid & Lower Back Pain-** Back problems are common for most gymnasts. Yoga helps to strengthen and align the spine which may help cure and prevent back problems.

These are just some of the many injuries and aches a gymnast may experience. Because gymnastics is one of the most challenging and difficult sports out there, with it comes greater possibility for mistakes and injuries. Practice the recovery poses in this chapter especially if you are injured, but also incorporate them into your regular practice if you feel inclined. They are great for restoring even a healthy body

A recovery style of yoga is considered more Yin Yoga. Yin is the opposite of yang, so it is much slower, softer, and gentle. In Yin and Restorative Yoga, you will hold poses anywhere from 2-20 minutes per side, and use props to support your body. Holding a pose for more than a minute really allows the body to restore and heal. The connective tissue and skeleton have time and space to rebuild. The mind has time to settle and let go.

If you are injured, or coming back from an injury, follow the same guidelines in Chapter 7 for developing a practice. Always begin with a 2-5 minute meditation, complete the poses you choose to practice, then end in Savasana for 5-10 minutes. Make sure to practice everyday for quicker recovery. Just like anything else, what you put in, you get out.

You are in the beginning stages of your injury, the best thing to do for yourself is rest, R & R is vital, even to the healthiest of bodies, so take advantage of your injury and totally rest. Sometimes the best thing for an injured body is straight up stillness. Meditation would be perfect. This would be a great time to develop and increase the power of the most important muscle in your body- the mind. Meditate, meditate, and then meditate some more. Review Chapter 3, Meditation, to get you started.

If you've had a severe injury and won't be back to gymnastics for a while, see which Recovery Poses would be best for you and work on them the best you can. You should be able to do at least half of the poses in this next section for most injuries. The poses will help your blood circulation, calm your nervous system, release toxins, and shift energy to a healthier frequency by balancing hormones and other functions of the body, and mind. Remember, in all of our poses, we can use as much or as little muscular energy to add more or less intensity to the practice. Now, let's roll out your mat to recovery!

RECLINED PIGEON
BUDDHA SQUAT
WIDE KNEE
CHILD POSE
ON BOLSTER
SIDE
CHILDS
TWIST WITH
BOLSTER

RECLINED PIGEON POSE

Reclined Pigeon is a modified pose for Pigeon Pose in Chapter 6. It is great for our emotional "storage-house", our hips.

1. Lie on your back and place the outer edge of you right foot on top of your bent left knee.
2. Grab under your left knee with both hands (right hand comes in between legs to reach under).
3. Bend right elbow back into right knee to push it out as much as feels good.
4. Keep both of your feet active to protect knee joints.
5. Find your mountain, find your drishti, and find your breath.
6. Stay in for up to 5 minutes and repeat on the other side.

BUDDHA SQUAT- SEAT AND HEELS ON BLANKET

This is a great pose for overall stability; it is great for grounding and calming your body and mind. It is great for releasing tension in the hips and lower back.

1. Set up a folded blanket, step your heels onto blanket, and squat down
2. Your seat will come all the way down onto the blanket. Adjust height of blanket as needed. Add another blanket if needed.
3. Take palms together in front of your heart.
4. Yourelbows will push into inner knees as you lengthen your spine.
5. Find your mountain, find your drishti, and find your breath.
6. Stay in for up to 5 minutes.

WIDE KNEE CHILDS POSE WITH BOLSTER

Child's pose is a great pose for your entire nervous system. Being in it sends signals to the body to relax, restore, and heal. Supported by a bolster gives the body full relief to surrender and let go. Enjoy for as long as you'd like! Take often...

1. Place a bolster or a few folded blankets on your mat.
2. Come down on your knees and place knees to the outside of the bolster as you come into Child's Pose.
3. Arms can rest on or off bolster. Find a position that is most relaxing to you.
4. Forehead can be down or switch between lying the right ear and left ear down.
5. Completely relax, let everything go, and find your drishti and breath.
6. Hold for up to 20 minutes.

SIDE CHILDS TWIST (WITH BOLSTER)

This supported twist is excellent for deep relaxation while the body restores in an invigorating pose for the spine and digestive system. Try turning the head to each side for a deeper or more relaxed posture. Soak in and enjoy!

1. Place a bolster or a few folded, stacked blankets on your mat.
2. Come down on your knees so that the end of the bolster is to the right of you and legs out to the side.
3. Lie on the bolster, belly down, left ear to bolster, and come into your twist, deepening it depending which way you gaze.
4. Play around with arm positions to find the most comfortable for you.
5. Completely relax, let everything go, find your drishti and find you breath.
6. Hold for up to 10 minute and repeat on the other side.

SUPPORTED PIGEON
SHOULDER OPENER
WITH A BLOCK
LEGS UP A WALL
SUPPORTED
SHOULDER
STAND
AGAINST WALL

SUPPORTED PIGEON

Move into this pose very mindfully. When you open your hips, this allows relief in your lower back, legs, blood flow, and more. If you can keep your hips open during your injury, you will be a step ahead on your road to recover. Hips are a store house for pain and tension (stuck energy) so keep them flexible.

1. Place a bolster or a few folded, stacked blankets on the ground in front of you.
2. Carefully come into Pigeon Pose over the bolster.
3. You will align the thigh with the side of the bolster, and the front leg will come off the front.
4. The floor or blocks will support your arms.
5. Completely relax, let everything go. Rest and enjoy.
6. Find your drishti and your breath.
7. Hold for up to 10 minutes and repeat on other side.

SHOULDER OPENER WITH BLOCK AGAINST A WALL

Gymnastics is one of the toughest sports on your body. Most gymnasts are known to have very tight shoulders. If you have a lower body injury take advantage of this time to work on opening and strengthening your shoulders.

1. Place a block next to the wall.
2. Come onto your knees facing the block and wall.
3. Place your elbows on the block, palms will be together, fingers up.
4. Wriggle your head in between your arms and place your forehead on the block.
5. Completely relax, let everything go, find your drishti, and find your breath.
6. Hold for up to 5 minutes.

LEGS UP THE WALL

Having your legs up a wall gives the heart and brain a rest as the blood is pumped towards them. This gives these organs a chance to restore, rest, and heal. This pose is great for overall health, and also great for when you can't sleep.

1. Lie on the floor so your legs and seat bones are up against a wall.
2. Legs will be straight but relaxed (optional: place a weighted bean bag across your feet)
3. Arms are wherever feels most comfortable.
4. Completely relax, let everything go, find your drishti and find your breath.
5. Hold for up to 20 minutes.

SUPPORTED SHOULDER STAND AGAINST A WALL

This is probably one of the best poses you can do out of all of the poses in this book, depending on your injury of course. But even if you are not injured, this pose is a must to include in your daily or at least weekly routine. This pose provides overall balance and stability.

1. Begin with your legs up a wall. Bend knees and bring feet flat to the wall.
2. Press your feet into the wall until your hips are stacked over your shoulders, and your knees over your hips. Arms will support your low back as you lift each vertebrae off the ground.
3. You will be able to tuck your shoulders under you more with the support of the wall.
4. You should feel no pressure in your neck. You can use a folded blanket under your shoulders like we do for regular Shoulder stand.
5. Calves will be parallel to the floor. You are striving towards creating a rectangle shape between your body and the wall.
6. Completely relax, let everything go, find your drishti and breath. Relax and enjoy.
7. Hold for up to 10 minutes and counter pose with Fish Pose.

SUPPORTED
BRIDGE POSE
RECLINED SEAT
RECLINED RESTING
ON BOLSTER
RECLINED RESTING ON BLOCK

SUPPORT BRIDGE POSE

This is a great modification to bridge pose. You will follow all of the principles of bridge pose but use the support of the block to allow you to open the heart and chest more so you can breathe fuller. This pose relaxes your entire mind and body.

1. Start lying on your back.
2. Bend knees and place feet on the floor hip width apart.
3. Press into your feet and place a block under your lower back. Make sure there is no pain in your back. It should feel completely comfortable. If not, play with the direction of the block.
4. Once the block feels centered, place your arms back down to your sides. Roll shoulders under you to open your heart and chest for maximum air flow.
5. Completely relax, let everything go, find your drishti, and find your breath.
6. Hold for up to 10 minutes.

RECLINED SEAT (SUPTA BADDHA KONASANA)

Reclined Seat is one of the best restorative poses you will ever take. It is the king of restorative poses. Sit back and watch the magic happen. The longer you hold the better!

1. Lie back so your entire back body lays on the ground.
2. Take the soles of your feet together and use blocks or pillows to support your knees if needed.
3. Arms will be placed off to your sides comfortably, palms up.
4. Completely relax, let everything go, find your drishti and find your breath.
5. Hold for up to 30 minutes, or more!

RECLINED RESTING POSE ON BOLSTER

Okay, so maybe this one is a tie for king of restorative yoga poses. Lying in this restorative position is great right before bed, or anytime during the day that you feel like you just need to unwind. It resets the entire body, bringing everything back into total balance.

1. Place a bolster or a few folded, stacked blankets on your mat.
2. Sit with one end of the bolster behind your lower back.
3. Lie back so your entire back and head are on the bolster; seat will remain on the floor.
4. Arms will be placed off to the sides comfortably, palms up, or however comfortable).
5. Completely relax, let everything go, find your drishti and find your breath,
6. Hold for up to 30 minutes.

(For an added bonus, to lengthen the spine and open hips even more, use a strap that is in a loop and have it around your waist with enough slack so it can also wrap around the outside edges of your feet. This will create a nice lengthening action, especially in the lower back area.)

RECLINED RESTING POSE ON BLOCK

Lying in this restorative position on a block right between the shoulder blades feels like heaven. For some it might not feel so hot though. Test it out. If it's not for you, then skip this pose. Remember, there's no yoga police. Or there shouldn't be anyway! Be mindful when going into this pose. It gets right into that hard to get space, your rhomboid, the meaty area between your shoulders, a tight spot for many. Apply the your body weight to this area can be beneficial to your entire body.

1. Place the block on your mat so that when you lay down it goes right between your shoulder blades. Play around with the height of the block and the exact area that the block hits the upper back. When you find that sweet spot you will know!
2. Your head and upper shoulders should remain on the floor.
3. Arms will be placed off to the sides, palms up or down.
4. Completely relax, let everything go, find your drishti, and find your breath. (Legs have option to go into Bodakonasana-soles of feet together, knees out to the sides).
5. Hold for up to 30 minutes.

An injury does not have to be all that bad. Look at it as having more time to learn something new and discover more about your intelligent body. You can literally learn to heal your own body using your own body. Take advantage of all of the information out there, especially online, about self-healing. While you are recovering, take the time to strengthen your mental muscle. Meditate, meditate, meditate! The residual effects of this will be amazing and help you out in the long run tremendously. Strengthening the mind's muscle through the practice of yoga, while you are injured, will increase your focus and concentration and will skyrocket you back into your practice once you're ready to start practicing again. You will come back even stronger and more prepared. Ready to conquer the world!

Try not to look at any "set-back" as a set back. Let it just be part of your journey. Except it for what it is and practice what you can each day. Each day you do your absolute best, no matter what the circumstances, is a successful day. Take each day as a lifetime. Each day *is* a new life. Don't take anything for granted and enjoy the ride.

CHAPTER 8

Calming Your Nerves

"The breath is the anchor for the mind. Pull in your mind with the breath. It is the mind that creates those butterflies. Learn to control the mind and that peace and calm that's always with you will shine through."

Jill Fox

Your palms are sweaty, knees weak, arms are heavy...you feel the butterflies in the stomach, maybe you're even a little nauseas, your heart is racing and your mind is going a thousand miles a minute... Your nerves can make it feel like you have a little hurricane running through your body. If you've been in a gymnastics meet, you probably know exactly what I am talking about. The nerves are one of the biggest obstacles that get in a gymnasts way during competitions or practice.

By mentally preparing yourself before a competition hours, the night before, or even days in advance, you will notice a significant difference in the way you feel and perform during a competition. This will not only be good for your routines and scores, but also for your entire well-being. Some nerves are good. They keep you feeling alive and can sometimes motivate you. It's the nerves that block us that we need to learn to control. Through consistent practices in this book, you should be able to walk into your competitions with nerves of steel.

Learning how to work with your breath will be one of the most effective things you can do to help calm you down during any situation. Try out some pranayama practices from Chapter 2 that you can do before a meet in a quiet space. Then throughout the competition, focus on making your exhales about a second or two longer. This will send a signal to the brain to calm down and relax you. Inhale, and count to four, exhale and count to six. Repeat this whenever you feel the nerves sneaking back in.

You could also pick a yoga sequence from Chapter 7 to practice the night before and leading into competition. The way you feel after a yoga class can have a lingering effect that may last for hours afterward. So practice the morning of the competition and feel the lasting affects later that day! A flow of even ten minutes will help to balance your body and mind.

These are also some other things you can do the night before the competition to help you be better prepared and more alert when you wake up the day of the meet:

PROPER SLEEP- Seems obvious, but proper sleep gets often overlooked. The night before a competition, make sure you are getting at least seven to eight hours of solid sleep. You want to be totally rested so that you are as alert and coherent as possible. When we don't get enough sleep, we do not function as efficiently; our reflexes are weaker, and we are less alert.

VISUALIZATION- There is a lot of power in visualizing yourself doing your skills and routines perfectly, over and over. Imagine yourself at your competition performing your routines perfectly- see yourself on the vault, running, feel the carpet under your feet, feel your hair blowing back as you run, feel yourself spring off the vault board, onto the vault, and stick your landing.

Put as much detail and thought into this as you lie there imagining yourself doing your perfect routines. The more details you have, the better. Your body and muscles will process and remember this information. Visualize your body into thinking, feeling, and seeing, as if you were already doing your routines perfectly.

COFFEE MEDITATION- Coffee Meditation is the most powerful thing you can do the night before your competition to improve your performance. It is also the most powerful thing you can do to improve your entire next day. It is done right before you fall asleep, and it is so important to enter this field of your day, our deepest, most unconscious state, in a calm and happy way. The field right after is where we are for a third of our lives. Even though it appears that we are doing nothing during these seven hours or so, this is when *so* much is going on. This is where the body restores itself, gets to completely surrender, and prepare for the next days challenges.

To do Coffee Meditation is very simple. As you lie there and go to sleep all you do is think really good thoughts. Do your visualization routines, but then right after those, as you are drifting off to sleep, think of all of the good things that you did that day, especially if you've done something to help someone.

Maybe you held a door open for somebody, or smiled at someone who looked like they needed it. Maybe you prayed for somebody. No matter how big or small, think of your good deeds from the day. Entering sleep this way offers the body a healthy state, gives the mind more ease for happier dreams, leaves you feeling more rested, and you wake up less tense, and more charged and inspired. Coffee meditation is learning to let go and trust you are supported by the great Source around and in you. Do your absolute best each day, enjoy life, and each moment when you lay your head down to sleep, know you are worthy.

Remember, when it does come time for the competition the only person you should really be competing against is yourself. All you can do is fully prepare yourself by training hard at practices, giving it your all, and being positive. No matter what happens though, it is important to be okay with it. Let go of the need for the gold medal, or the embarrassment of the three falls on beam, and move on to the next day. Each day is a new life, so don't let a bad or good day define you.

What does define you is your attitude when the going gets tough, or even when the going gets good. Being able to let go of the outcome of a situation in life is going to help free you from a lot of struggle. Try not to attach to certain titles, outcomes, or opinions. As long as you have a clear intention, are doing your best with what you have today, stay true to yourself, and give your best attitude and effort, and then outcomes should never matter.

Don't get hung up on a score, a fall, how your coach feels, judges, or any of your regrets or choices in life. Learn to accept what happened and let go of the outcomes. If you don't, they will drag you down. Learn to with the flow. Life is full of ups and downs; it always will be. Stay flexible in mind and body!

CHAPTER 9

Happy Thoughts & Intentions

"Everything is energy and that's all there is to it. Match the frequency of the reality you want and you can not help to get that reality. It can be no other way. This is not philosophy. This is physics."
EINSTEIN

The thoughts you think are like little seeds; each and every thought, dream, desire, every word you speak; each of these holds energy that eventually springs to life and is creating your world around you. This is where our concentration and mindfulness learned through yoga and meditation come in handy. When we learn how to think good thoughts, a.k.a. *plant good seeds*, we are creating an energetic frequency around ourselves that attracts positive things back to us. It's literally like planting a garden and watching its' fruits grow.

We plant our gardens by the things that we say, do, or think. These actions create a rippling affect out into the world, especially in your own lives, and to those lives nearest and dearest to us. What you say, do, or think really does affect every person around you. There is an invisible thread that connects you to every living being, person, animal, tree, star, and speck of sand around you whether you believe it or not. This *is **why prayer and mantras are so powerful. When we focus on something with utmost*** **attention**, it sparks a flame just as a seed is sparked to sprout. Think about it- have you ever thought about a song and then next thing you know it comes on the radio? This happens quite often, doesn't it?

Depending on what we are thinking can affect whether we feel good or bad. We can't always be in a good mood but when we're not, we can always try positive thoughts and intentions to try to turns things around. Through intentional thought, you can shift how you feel almost instantly. The body and mind can't tell the difference if we believe, or if we make-believe. The mind is so powerful that the body will believe whatever it tells us

So, as I was saying earlier, attitude and hard work are vital factor in achieving your goals, but you need to put the work in to get a great outcome, point blank. That's just how it goes, and how it will always go in the end in every area of your life. Sure there are some individuals who may have natural talent and seem to excel in a breeze, but if they don't put the hard work in, natural talent will only take them so far. The hard workers will end up passing them down the road.

It will be hard to keep the fire for working towards a goal without an intention. An intention gives purpose. It's what's important to you and what makes you tick. Intentions give reasons to what you do. Without a reason what would be the point? Get very clear on what it is you want in life. This question will come up over and over for you again. How far do you want to go in gymnastics? What do you want to be when you grow up? What do you live for? What is the why behind all that you do?

We need to be clear on exactly what our goals are. Most people never really attain their goals because they never had very clear ones to begin with. You need to be able to see, touch, feel, taste, and hear it. We need to believe it with all of our being and do what we can each day to work towards that dream or goal.

Everything important that you do in your life should have an intention behind it, a why. Pick something that you really want to accomplish in gymnastics, or in your life. Seeing, feeling, and imagining as if it were already true is the best way to manifest your goals. This is one of the greatest secrets to actually bringing your dreams into fruition.

Take a moment and write about one of your goals here. Use as much detail as possible:

Journaling is a good way to help us connect to our intentions and ourselves. A journal can be kept in a number of different ways- fictional, non-fictional, lists, stories, notes, letters, and doodles. There are innumerable ways and anyway is good. Whatever feels fun, free, natural, and non-stressful to you. Writing can be very meditative and helps to get us out of our heads and organize our thoughts so that they might become clearer and more understood.

Writing about your dreams and goals keeps an ignited spark fresh inside of you. It helps to make sense of some of the mind. It keeps your brain exercised and your creative juices flowing. You will notice that the things you write about in your journal are the things closest to your heart. If your not sure of your intentions or goals, journaling is a sure fire way to help you figure that out.

Use a journal to set a time frame for when you want to attain your goal. Do what you can with what you have in the time and space you are currently in. Baby steps are a good pace. Try to not get overwhelmed by the actual goal. It's too much to think of the dream or goal in terms of the final stage. The largeness of their dreams tends to scare most people away. If you want to learn a double back, it could be overwhelming to think about the double back if we don't even have our back flips yet. This can detour someone because the idea is just too big. Think about your goals in terms of what you can do little by little thoug in order to move closer to your goals. Narrow it down by taking your goals in strides. Go month-to-month, or week-to-week, even day to day, depending on the goal. In no time you will be will on your way to conquering your dreams. Time flies when you're having fun!

CHAPTER 10

Diet & Nutrition

"If people knew how badly animals are treated in today's factory farms, if people knew how completely confined and immobilized these creatures are for their entire lives, if people know how severe and unrelenting is the cruelty these animals are forced to endure, there would be change. If people knew. But too many of us choose to look the other way, to keep the veil in place, to remain unconscious and caught in the cultural trance. That way we are more comfortable. That way is convenient. That way we don't have to risk too much. This is how we keep ourselves asleep"

–John Robbins

You are what you eat, literally. Eating is a very sacred communion between you and your body. Besides the breath, food is the most intimate thing you will ever experience in your body. Just like most things, the food we eat, and lifestyles we live, are not a one size fits all formula. What some of us need to fuel and function is not what everyone else needs. Just like every other choice in your lifetime you will make, check in with yourself and make the best possible choice according to YOU. Eating healthy affects our mind, body, hair, sight, skin, and nails; plus, our muscles, bones, blood, mind, focus, and more.

Eating healthy is one of the pillars in yoga. It is something to be looked at very seriously. Our food can become our medicine or a part of our ailment. It can make us sicker or healthier. Our health depends very much on the types of food, amount of food, and the quality of food that we eat. We literally are what we eat. Eating foods that come directly from the Earth is a good way to know you are getting nutrient dense foods. That is, if the food came from an un-contaminated part of the Earth. Organic food is the best kind of food you can eat. Organic means the food has come from a part of the Earth where there have been no added chemicals or pesticides to the soil or plant.

Try to cut way back on processed foods. Processed foods are mostly anything that is in a box or package. Also look out for GMO's (genetically modified organisms) in your food. These are cells that have been modified by genetic engineering. There is not enough research as to what this manipulation can do to your mind or body so it is best to steer clear of them for now. They are not currently labeled, an ironically so do not have to be, so look for foods that are labeled *non-GMO*.

In yoga philosophy we should fill our belly's with half solid food, a quarter fluids, and the other quarter air. We don't want to overstuff ourselves. We want to make sure that we are getting the right balance of whole foods and nutrients. Knowing at least a little about pure foods and healthy food choices is important to maintaining a healthy body and mind. Also make sure that the water you are drinking is healthy. Most people trust their tap water, but if that's what you drink make sure it has been tested by a professional. A Berkey Water Filter is a good route to go if your city water is not good.

Eating with the Seasons

The types of food you will eat throughout the year should change due to the fact that what's available from nature will change. You should be eating lots of whole foods from nature daily. Just by looking around outside you can learn the basics about the types of food you should be eating.

If you are ever in doubt about what to eat each season, head on down to your local farmers market and see what they have on hand. What your farmers have to offer is what is available that season. Buying direct from a farmer is the very best way to go. It gives the farmer a better return for his hard earned work, and you get to see first hand where your hard earned money is going. It is better for the environment, and your food will be the freshest.

Spring Eating

Imagine it's springtime- the birds are chirping, the bees and bugs come out to play, the soil softens, little sprouts begin to shoot and buds begin to form. There is a lot you can do with certain sprouts, shoots, and weeds. For instance, did you know that a dandelion is a weed is actually good for you? You can make tea out of the roots by picking, cleaning, and boiling them. The tea helps to promote digestion, helps clean kidneys, and more. (Recipe follows later in the chapter)

There are many leafy greens and tender vegetables available in the spring. Get your friends together and go outside to see what you can find. 'Foraging', is gathering plants from outside to use for food. Never put anything in your mouth that you are uncertain of; do your research! There is nutrition all around you. Springtime is also a perfect time to grow your own food and start a garden. Even if you don't have a lot of land, plant a couple tomato plants or strawberry plants in pots. Just to have one or two plants growing in your kitchen or on your patio will bring in a breath of fresh air!

Incorporate these foods into your diet in the springtime:

Apricots
Arugula
Artichokes
Asparagus
Avocados
Carrots
Chives
Dandelion
Leeks
Mangoes
Peas
Pineapples
Potatoes
Rhubarb
Spinach
Sprouts

Summer Eating

In the summertime, we want to eat cooling foods and drink more water since we are usually more active in the summer months, and also since the sun can dehydrate our bodies. Try to stick to water, as opposed to juices and sodas. Make iced teas, or flavor your waters with different fruits and herbs. (Recipes follow later in this chapter).

You should drink between eight to twelve glasses of water a day. Not drinking enough water can make you feel fatigued. Make sure the water is good, clean, drinking water, and try to avoid buying plastic water bottles. These are terrible on the environment! San Francisco just became the first city in America to completely ban plastic water bottles. You can buy a water bottle and refill it often throughout your day- stainless steel is the best. First thing you should do when waking up is drink a warm cup of water with lemon. The water helps to neutralize and recharge the body after a nights sleep, and is easier on the body first thing as opposed to cold water.

Masaru Emoto was a Japanese researcher who studied water extensively. He believed that water was a blueprint for our reality, and that there is way more to it than what meets the eye. He studied the molecules in water and how they would change shape during different situations. For instance, when different styles of music were playing, or when people were thinking or talking in certain ways, the water molecules were influenced by changing shapes. When heavy metal music played the molecules would shrink and become more rigid or sharp edged. When classical music played, the molecules would expand into beautiful, curvy, peaceful shapes. If we are made up of 80 percent water, imagine how the water in our bodies are being influenced by our thoughts, words, and actions.

Incorporate these foods into your diet in the summertime:

Avocado	Green Beans	Potatoes
Broccoli	Lemons	Strawberries
Beets	Melons	Raspberries
Figs	Oranges	Tomatoes
Grapes	Peaches	

Autumn Eating

In autumn, we turn to warmer foods such as potatoes, onions, and carrots. As the summer comes to an end and the leaves begin to fall, we tend to physically and mentally do the same. It is helpful to remember this so you don't feel like something is wrong with you during this time. A lot of people may feel like they are tired or feeling down in autumn, when actually, your body is saying to rest and take it easy, just as nature does. When seasons change so do we. Leaves fall and our energy starts to fall. Begin to notice when seasons change how your energy shifts.

Our days get shorter in the autumn. The sun rises earlier and sets later. Try to adjust your sleep schedule also as the seasons change. This is a good time to add warmer foods to your diet to keep your inner thermo system strong. Drink more teas and eat more soups. Autumn is crockpot season, so try experimenting with making homemade soups. They are very comforting to eat and make the home smell so good! (Recipes later in chapter.)

Incorporate these foods into your diet in the fall time:

Almonds	Olives	Squash
Apples	Pears	Sweet Potato
Dates	Peppers	Walnuts
Figs	Persimmons	
Limes	Pomegranate	

Winter Eating

In winter, turn to even more warming foods such as eggs, squash, and root vegetables. Soups are still a great thing to keep in your diet in the winter and a great way to pack a lot of nutrients in one bowl. This is a time of year that is common for most people to gain a few extra pounds, especially with all of the holidays; food is everywhere! This is a time to be cautious of sugar. Make mindful choices. Don't over indulge but don't hold back either. A few cookies will not hurt you and the body will appreciate a little extra cushion for warmth during this cold winter season. Never deprive yourself! Simply find a healthy balance.

Incorporate these foods into your diet in the wintertime:

Artichoke	BrusselSprout	Grapefruits	Parsnips
Pumpkin	Kohlrabi	Mandarins	Turnips

Vegetarianism

Ahimsa, you may recall, means *non-harming*. Patanjali says if you do not cause suffering upon any being physically, mentally, or vocally eventually you will be freed from suffering. Cutting back, or eliminating meat from your diet, may lessen the suffering in the world caused to other beings. Vegetarianism is very healthy for your body and the planet. Simply cutting out meat 1-day a week you can help to repair the Earth exponentially. 45% of total landmass in the United States is used for animal farming.

Over half of the grains that we grow are fed to livestock while millions of people are starving. The country's most grown food to feed livestock is corn and soybeans, and these are linked to more topsoil erosion than any other crop. Because we house so many animals in one space through factory farming, the soil is also being highly contaminated from toxic manures due to the chemicals and hormones given to the animals. These wastes then run off into our rivers, lakes, and streams, and eventually into our water systems, contaminating those too.

Watch the movies Fast Food Nation and Forks Over Knives. These movies are a bit older do a good job of at least opening your eyes to some of the terrible food practices out there. From there you be inspired to learn even more. When I first became a vegetarian at the age of thirteen I was given the book Diet for a Small Planet, which is a great place to also start. Although that was back in 1992 and it may not be totally up to date by now, this is a very good read. Today there is a plethora of resources available. Check out the library or local bookstore for some of the latest books.

Do your research to make sure you are getting the proper nutrients your body needs before making any drastic changes to your diet. You'll want to know which foods to eat to get all of the vitamins and minerals you need to maintain a healthy physical body. Eat a wide variety of foods nutrient dense, organic, raw, natural foods. By sticking to the seasonal foods that come from the Earth, you should be well on your way to eating the proper nutrition that your body desires for a healthy life.

50 Vegetarian Foods to Add to Your Diet:

1. Avocado
2. Apples
3. Almonds
4. Barley
5. Basil
6. Bananas
7. Barley
8. Basil
9. Blueberries
10. Beans
11. Beets
12. Brown Rice
13. Broccoli
14. Brussels Sprouts
15. Cantaloupe
16. Carrots
17. Cashews
18. Cheese
19. Cinnamon
20. Collard Greens
21. Cranberries
22. Cauliflower
23. Dates
24. Flax Seed
25. Figs
26. Garlic
27. Grapes
28. Grapefruit
29. Kale
30. Kiwis
31. Lentils
32. Lemons
33. Nuts
34. Onions
35. Oranges
36. Pasta
37. Papaya
38. Pineapple
39. Prunes
40. Quinoa
41. Raspberries
42. Seeds
43. Sprouts
44. Stone Fruits
45. Sweet Potatoes
46. Tempeh
47. Tofu
48. Tomatoes
49. Watermelon
50. Yogurt

Ayurveda

Ayurveda is one of the oldest medicinal systems in the world. Ayurveda takes into account a number of factors to determine what foods and medicines are best for a person to be balanced in mind and body. It is not a 'one-size fits all' approach, which can often be found in the West. We get to the root of the problems as opposed to the surface with Ayurveda. Instead of prescribing medicine as a first source, many things are tested, or ruled out, to help find a solution to the cure.

In Ayurveda, doctors take into account that all people are different based on many factors- where, when, and to whom a person is born, what the person's environment was like, the persons DNA and genes, and more. So many things go into making up who we are. Ayurveda is a scientific system that helps find a person's unique constitution, and based on that, they will know what diet, times of day, time of year, temperatures, setting, paces, styles, and more are best for them.

There are three "rhythms" (a.k.a. doshas) and each of us has a dominant dosha. Our dosha balances us and help us determine what we can do to live our life to our fullest and healthiest. Learning simple things such as types of food to eat, and times of day that are best for your type to eat them, can be a game changer for sure.

The three doshas are:

1. Pitta- controls bodies metabolism, such as body temperature and digestion.
2. Kapha- controls growth in the body and maintains the immune system.
3. vata- controls movements such as blinking, heart beating, and breathing.

Each type, depending on which is your dominant trait, will determine things for you such as which temperatures you do best in, or if spicy or non spicy foods are good for you, or if you do your best thinking in the morning or evening. According to your constitution, you will be able to follow more accurate diets and lifestyle routines to help you feel and be your best at all times.

One the next page is a simple test you can do to help you determine what your possible dosha, or constitution is so you can start to incorporate foods into your diet that are designed for your body type.

BODY SIZE	THIN______	MEDIUM______	LARGE______
WEIGHT	LOW______	MEDUIM______	HIGH______
SKIN	DRY______	SMOOTH______	OILY______
HAIR	DRY______	STRAIGHT______	THICK______
NOSE	UNEVEN______	LONG______	SHORT______
NAILS	DRY______	SHARP______	THICK______
LIPS	DRY______	CHAPPED______	SMOOTH______
NECK	THIN______	MEDIUM______	LARGE______
BELLY	SMALL______	MEDIUM______	LARGE______
APPETITE	IRREGULAR______	HUNGRY______	REGULAR______
PERSONALITY	OUTGOING______	ABMITIOUS______	RELAXED______
SLEEP	SHORT______	MEDIUM______	DEEP______

As you can see, a lot goes in to determining your unique dosha. Put only one check mark next to the thing that relates to you most. If you find it hard to decide just do your best to determine what is most like you. If you ever have a professional Ayurvedic consultation be prepared to be asked many questions like these to help determine your constitution. The column that has the most amount of check marks will help determine which dosha is most in balance with you. This isn't a conclusive test, but it will give you a good idea. If you want to learn more about your constitution and how to apply it to your life, you will be able to find plenty of information online.

**Use the result from the test above to start researching more about your dominant dosha. Begin incorporating what you have learned and see if you notice any positive energetic, mental, or physical shifts.*

Eating Disorders and Mindful Eating

Gymnasts have one of the highest rates of eating disorders compared to other athletes. The constant pressure to stay a certain size and weight adds to this rate. A gymnast, once they get to a certain level, are usually told they need to remain a certain weight and are weighed in. The problem is most gymnasts are not properly taught how to fuel their bodies. This lack of education around proper diet can turn some gymnasts to eating disorders in fear of getting fat.

More people suffer from some sort of eating disorder then you may think. Whether they are addicted to sugar, eat too much or too little, or become obsessed with their weight, most people have probably struggled with food at one point or another in their lives. If you are struggling with an eating disorder reach out to someone. You will be surprised how common they really are. You are not alone.

The state of mind we are in while we are eating is very important and can affect how the food is absorbed and digested into our bodies. We want to open all of our senses to the food when we are chewing. When we eat mindfully we then taste, hear, smell, feel, and absorb the food better. The body appreciates it more and this leaves us with a feeling of satisfaction and fulfillment. Eating this way also helps to stabilize mood and empower the mind.

Make sure you chew your food well. You've probably heard this a million times but you should take about thirty chews per bite to help break down the enzymes of the food before swallowing. The food becomes more enjoyable, your food will be digested better, and it's easier on the body. This also helps us to slow down the process of eating instead of just shoving food down and hurrying onto our next endeavor.

Aly Raisman, on an Overshare episode, says that 'when she looks in the mirror she picks out the good things she sees about herself instead of the bad things.' Practice this! Whenever you stand in front of the mirror, talk and look nicely at yourself. Recognize all of the amazing unique qualities that make you- you! Write it on your mirror in lipstick to remind yourself. The things that will always make you most beautiful are your attitude and your confidence. How you feel on the inside will reflect how you look on the outside. Never forget that. Beauty radiates from the inside out.

Most of the reasons we develop such bad relationships between our foods and our bodies is because our mind, body, and Spirit are disconnected. Practicing meditation, yoga, mindfulness, and forming a better relationship with your food and body can play a huge and dramatic role in helping your relationship with food.

There are many things you can do to help improve your health and quality of living: Eat whole, organic, local foods as much as possible. Use beauty products that are natural and organic. Meditate and do yoga everyday. Keep a positive attitude about yourself and life. Be grateful and compassionate towards all beings. Make sure you are getting outdoors every day. Take your shoes off once in awhile and let the soles of your feet connect with the dirt and grass. Maybe even choose to do your meditations outdoors once and a while. The more we connect with nature, the more we stay grounded. Take a hike through the woods, put your feet in the sand, swim in an ocean or lake, lie in the grass and look up at the clouds, bird watch, or climb a tree. Mother nature is one of the most healing medicines and she is always available to you. Don't take her for granted.

Here are an array of drinks and snacks that you can experiment with that are power packed with nutrients. Hopefully they will inspire you to add more nutrient-dense, whole foods to your diet. Remember, do your best to buy local, organic produce and foods whenever possible!

Recipes

Smoothies

Smoothies are a great way to get lots of nutrients in one cup, especially first thing in the morning. They are the perfect breakfast! You don't need an expensive blender to make a good smoothie either. One on the cheaper end will work just fine. There are a million different combinations you can us. Below are some ideas for bases, mixers, liquids, and extras you can add to create your own favorite blends; as well as recipes.

Bases- Yogurt or frozen bananas (take out of freezer about 5-10 minutes before blending frozen bananas)

Mixers- Fresh or frozen fruits (or both), strawberries, raspberries, dates, kale, spinach, carrots, mangoes, blueberries, coconut, peaches, etc.

Liquids-Water, tea, milks (cows, almond, rice, coconut, hemp, etc.), fresh juices

Extras- Peanut butter, flax seeds, hemp seeds, chia seeds, ginger, turmeric, cinnamon, other spices and herbs, honey, probiotics

Thin Mint

2 cups almond milk, unsweetened
1 ½ cups fresh spinach
½ cup fresh mint leaves
2 bananas
½ avocado
4 medjool dates, pitted
2 tablespoons cacao powder
OPTIONAL: cacao nibs sprinkled on top

1. Blend spinach, mint, and almond milk until smooth.
2. Add remaining ingredients and blend until smooth. Enjoy!

Raspberry Coconut Shortcake

2 cups spinach
1 cup coconut milk
1 cup coconut water
3 cups raspberries
1 Tablespoon ground flax seed
1 teaspoon vanilla extract
(OPTIONAL: garnish with coconut flakes, flax seed)

1. Blend spinach and liquid until smooth.
2. Add remaining ingredients and blend until smooth. Garnish with coconut flakes and flax seed if you'd like. Enjoy!

Takes Two to Mango

2 cups fresh spinach
1 ½ cups water
2 cups frozen mango
1 orange, peeled
¼ cup rolled oats

1. Blend spinach, orange, and water until smooth.
2. Add remaining ingredients and blend until smooth. Enjoy!

Watermelon Slushies

Watermelon
Ice
Dash of Cinnamon
Fresh Mint (Optional)

1. Blend to desired consistency.
2. Enjoy!

Peanut Butter Banana Chocolate Almond Smoothie

Peanut Butter
Banana
Chocolate Almond milk
Dash of Salt

1. Blend and Enjoy!

Thirst Quenchers

We need at least six to eight glasses of water a day to get our energy up, stay properly hydrated, and for our bodies to run efficiently. Start each morning with a warm cup of lemon water. The lemon helps to alkaline the body. The warmer temperature is easier on the system than cold water when you first wake up. Probiotics are good to add in juice or water first thing also. You can buy probiotics at your local health food market. Try some of these other drinks below that will keep you hydrated, and refreshed, are so easy to make, and taste so good!

Let's start with flavored waters, then coconut and almond milk, then chai tea. All of which are very healthy and great to sip on throughout the days. Just like smoothies, there are a million different ways that you can make flavored water. The longer you soak the fruits, veggies, and/or hers and spices the more potent it will taste. Experiment with the amounts you use of each ingredient.

Start with any mix or blend of these ingredients to make your own unique blend!
FRUIT and VEGGIES- Cucumber, Apple, Strawberries, Raspberries, Lemon, Lime, Oranges, Melon, Beets, Pomegranates

HERBS and SPICES- Basil, Thyme, Lavender, Cinnamon, Ginger, Rosemary, Cocao Nibs

Honey Lemon Ginger Water

Honey
Lemon
Ginger

1. Boil water. Remove and add honey, juice from a lemon, and chopped ginger.
2. Enjoy!

Strawberry Basil Breeze Water

Strawberries
Basil
Lemon

1. For an entire pitcher: muddle the strawberries. Clean basil then add handful to pitcher. Squeeze an entire lemon or two in the pitcher.
2. Stir with wooden spoon and enjoy ☺

Cumcumber Apple Thyme Water

Cucumber
Apple
Fresh Thyme

1. Slice cucumbers and apples and toss them in pitcher or glass.
2. Clean thyme and add to pitcher.
2. Stir with wooden spoon and enjoy ☺

Lavender Honey Water

Fresh Lavender
Honey

1. Clean lavender and add to pitcher or glass. Add honey. Make sure honey is real. (honey can easily be disguised as corn syrup)
2. Stir and enjoy! ☺

Homemade Coconut or Almond Milk

Shredded Coconut or Raw Almonds (depending on if you are making coconut or almond milk)
Filtered Water

1. Place 1 to 2 cups of coconut or almonds in blender
2. Add water until it fills line on blender
3. Blend for a few minutes
4. Use a nut bag or cheesecloth to pour liquid into a pitcher.
   Might be less messy to pour into a bowl first and then transfer into a pitcher.
5. Reuse leftover coconut or almonds and add more water to repeat one or two more times. Use your best judgment to determine consistency and taste that's best for you.
6. Enjoy with homemade cookies ☺

Chai Tea

1 Cinnamon Stick
1-3 Star Anise
5-6 Cardamom Pods
5-6 Cloves (whole)
Fresh Ginger Root (thinly sliced, about an inch piece)
1 teaspoon whole black peppercorns
Black Tea (a few pinches of loose leaf or 1-2 teabags)

1. Simmer all ingredients for at least 10 minutes. The longer the stronger.
2. Turn off heat and add milk (whole, 2%, coconut, almond, etc.)
3. Add honey or brown sugar to taste!
4. Enjoy ☺

Salads

There are a million options to create a healthy salad. Salads are a great side, snack, or meal. When you make a salad, make it as colourful as possible. Use organic, fresh ingredients, and clean everything thoroughly. A salad spinner is a great investment if you don't have one. Here are some ideas you can add to your salads, and ideas for simple homemade dressings. Toss all of your choices together in a big Tupperware bowl, shake, and enjoy!

Start with any mix or blend of these ingredients to make your own unique blend!

GREENS- Kale, Spinach, Romaine Lettuce, Arugula, Cabbage, Swiss Chard, Iceberg Lettuce, Sprouts (try growing your own sprouts!)

SALAD MIXINGS- Carrot or Beet shavings, Cauliflower, Broccoli, Peppers, Onions, Green Onions, Potatoes, Tomatoes, Cucumber, Strawberries, Apples

SALAD FIXINGS- Nutritional Yeast, Hemp Seeds, Chia Seeds, Sunflower Seeds, Spices, Herbs, Edible Flower Petals, Cheese (Mozzarella, Parmesan, Cottage Cheese), Olives, Walnuts, Almonds, Raisins, Peas, Corn Tofu, Meat, Egg, Beans (Garbanzo, Black, Pinto)

DRESSINGS- Bragg's Amino Acids, Fresh Lemon, Olive Oil, Sesame Oil, Organic Dressings (Annie's Green Goddess Dressing is awesome!)

Power Snacks

Power snacks are foods we can eat throughout the day that are packed with nutrients and good energy, and that we don't have to feel guilty for enjoying. Did you know the definition of a 'calorie' is *energy?!* You want to be sure the calories you eat are good energy for your body and mind. Too much sugar and junk food can have a terrible effect on your mind. Many illnesses and diseases kids are getting is due to the diet they eat alone. Here are some recipes for healthy power snacks that are great for on the go. Something a busy gymnasts know all about!

Peanut Butter Filled Dates

Figs
Natural Peanut Butter (smooth or chunky)

1. Take pit out of the figs and cut a slit down the center
2. Fill with peanut butter
3. Enjoy!

Ants on a Beam

Raisins
Celery
Natural Peanut Butter

1. Clean celery and cut into desired lengths
2. Spread peanut butter evenly on celery
3. Place raisins in a row over peanut butter
4. Enjoy!

Homemade Vegan Ice Cream

Frozen Bananas
Desired Mix-Ins, such as: Peanut Butter, Cocao Nibs, Fruits, Dates, Nuts

1. Take frozen bananas out of the freezer and let sit for 10 minutes to thaw. They will blend better for you.
2. A food processor works best but a blender will work too. Pulse bananas until they are the consistency of ice cream.
3. Add in desired ingredients or add toppings.
4. Enjoy!

Hummus

Garbanzo Beans- 1 cup
Garlic- to taste
Olive Oil- 2 Tbsp
Lemon- juice from 1 lemon
Tahini- about ¼ cup (ground sesame seeds, found in most grocery stores)

1. Soak beans 8-24 hours (unless you are using can beans).
2. Cook beans about 2 hours until tender (unless using canned).
3. Blend all ingredients together to desired consistency.
4. Enjoy with crackers, pretzels, or veggies ☺.

Veggie Fries

Assorted Veggies, such as: Potatoes, Sweet Potatoes, Parsnips, and Carrots
Olive Oil
Salt (or other spices and herbs)

1. Clean and slice vegetables to resemble French Fries
2. Toss in olive oil and salt
3. Bake 450 degrees for approximately 25 minutes.
4. Enjoy! ☺

Other Good Quick Energy Snacks for On The Go:

- Pretzels
- Popcorn (options to add: nutritional yeast, coconut oil, cinnamon, Pink Himalayan Sea Salt)
- Rice Cakes
- Nuts
- Seeds
- Dried Fruit
- Hard Boiled Eggs
- Fresh Squeezed Juices
- Homemade Granola
- Greek Yogurt Parfaits
- Frozen Fruit Bars

Food is to be used for energy and fulfilment and less for enjoyment. Although we want to enjoy our food, we want to put health over pleasure. Remember the source in which your food came from, the way in which you eat, and why and how you are eating are important factors in your relationship with food. When we develop a healthy relationship with our food, we digest it better, enjoy and appreciate it more, feel more fulfilled, and are less susceptible to develop eating disorders or an unhealthy body.

Educate yourself about the harmful chemicals that can be in foods. Pay close attention to labels. Many of the labels can be quite deceiving. Did you know in many of the foods you eat there is something called GMO (genetically modified food), and the FDA doesn't even require that to be on a label?! A product labelled *natural* on it does not mean a product is completely natural. Products can still be labelled natural and still have chemicals in them. Do your research! We can be easily fooled…

Your taste buds will start to change the healthier you eat, and you may notice processed and junk foods will begin to taste just like what they are- junk! Keep your diet simple and add foods according to your dosha, what your community offers, and the seasons. Learn to eat healthy now and you will never have to go on any of those fad diets. You can just go on with your healthy lifestyle! By forming healthy habits now, you will notice that your mind is more alert and you have more energy. Your body will stabilize itself to maximize your fullest potential for your gymnastics training and for life.

CHAPTER 11

For the Coaches

"Whether you think you can or can't you are right"
HENRY FORD

This chapter is for the coaches. It is short and sweet, assuming you've read this entire book, you should have all the necessities to add yoga into your gymnasts training. Be sure you have read all of the chapters thoroughly to get the clearest understanding of how yoga works. To get the utmost knowledge and understanding of the power behind yoga you should roll your own mat out and get a taste of yoga for yourself. It is hard to taste something unless you really take a bit out of it! Once you have a clear understanding that yoga is more then stretching, you can take what you like from this book and implement it into your gymnastics practices for the recreational, pre-team, and team levels.

You don't have to be a yoga teacher to teach children yoga. As a coach, you already hold the knowledge of the importance of mind-body connection for your athletes. Add the cherries on top now with the teachings in this book to enhance your gymnasts potential. Teach them the power of their breath, the importance of keeping a positive mind (during and out of practice), and correct alignment (in mind, body, and breath). Watch them become more centered and grounded. Remind them to keep a calm, steady breath, often, throughout their practice.

Adding yoga to your coaching program is beneficial and vital for so many reasons. Starting to implement the yoga techniques at a young age will build better balance, concentration, cognitive function, emotional regulation, self-esteem, confidence, strength, mind and body connection, and more. Children will be able to calm down better, and make better decisions based on their improved awareness. We all know it can be difficult for younger kids to listen to instructions, which is a very important lesson in order for a gymnast to excel. Yoga improves and sharpens this focus very quickly for most children.

The best times to add yoga to your practices are when the gymnasts are warming up and stretching, during rotations as a filler rotation, or at the end when they are cooling down and stretching. Also, you may want to consider bringing in a yoga teacher and offering a full (at least 1-hour) yoga class (at least once a week) for your gymnasts or team. A cool down class on a Friday night, or a more energizing class first thing on Saturday mornings would be perfect for team girls each week. Plus incorporate at least 10 minutes a day into their practice.

Yoga *is* for every *body* and everybody, but the way in which we practice it is not one size fits all. The paths can each be a bit different, depending on age, caliber, mentality, body, injury, and more. Younger kids are going to have a harder time staying still and older kids are going to understand some of the yoga concepts a little bit faster. Yoga should be introduced differently according to age groups and gymnastics levels.

By incorporating some of these yoga practices into your gym, you will not only be creating better gymnasts, but you will be helping children. You will be surprised how much the parents will even appreciate it. The parents of my recreational gymnasts I coach have thanked me over and over for warming the girls up with 10 minutes of yoga! You are introducing such a vital skill into their child's life, a skill of living in their fullest potential, coming from a place within themselves, a place of centeredness and grounding.

We will start with some ideas you can incorporate into your recreational classes. Then, we will move into yoga for pre-team classes, and finally yoga for your team girls. Remember, that you will have different calibers of girls within each level. Some gymnasts might adapt and understand the concepts of yoga right away, while others will take more time. Be patient with both the gymnasts and yourself when bringing this new concept into their practice. It may take time to adjust just like anything else. Don't have too many expectations at first. If the children are not adapting to it one day let it go and come back to it the next day. In the end, this is just what yoga teaches us. Be patient, try again, stay positive, all will come.

***The warm-up exercises in this chapter can be used for all levels, and the Sun Salutations and poses are different for each level. They build off each other from the recreation to team level.**

Meditations for Recreational Gymnasts

Meditations will be shorter for recreational gymnasts. Start with anywhere from 30 seconds to 2 minutes. Their attention spans will be short so be patient with them and the practice. Use these simple meditation ideas below to begin practice. It is a great way to help the children shift energy from the outside world to inside the gym and into their bodies. (You will then move into warm-up poses, and then into Sun Salutations or other yoga poses, depending on the children and group.)

Ring a Bell

You can use a real bell, or a Tibetan chime. I love Tibetan Chimes, they have an incredible vibrational sound that radiates and echoes. You can also find a bell sound on iTunes, YouTube, or a phone app. You want the sound to linger. The point is to have the children hold their attention on the sound of the bell until it is completely gone. Notice how the sound linger for quite a while. You can repeat this two or three times depending on how well they are responding to it.

ENERGY FINGERS

While sitting in a pretzel seat, the children's hands will be in front of them, fingertips together. As they inhale have them expand their fingers. As they exhale, have them bend their fingers into a circle shape. They will look at hands for the first few breaths then have them close their eyes. As they inhale have them imagine they are blowing up a balloon (which is their lungs). As they exhale have them imagine the balloon losing air.

FIVE BREATHS

Have the children start by lying down or sitting in pretzel pose, depending on the group. Have them start by touching the thumbs to the index fingers. They will do one cycle of breath, both inhale and exhale, as they hold these fingers together. Then have them move the thumb to the middle finger for a cycle of breath. Repeat this down each finger with their eyes closed having them take their time and keeping the entire body still except for the finger's subtle movements.

STARING CONTEST

Have the children pick a partner or choose for them. A staring contest helps focus a child's mind as long as they are trying. This a a fun way to help bring a child turn inward. Let them have fun with it. At first they might giggle a lot but the more they practice, the more serious they will become.

MOUNTAIN BREATHS

The children will start standing in Mountain Pose. As they inhale, their arms will come up overhead, palms together. As they exhale, they will fold forward all the way bringing their hands to the floor. Have them inhale and repeat the entire sequence. Focus should be on connecting breath and movement, having a still focus, and steadiness in mind and body.

CLOUD POSE

Have the children will lay in Cloud 9 Pose (Savasana) and pretend that they are lying in a field of sunflowers watching clouds as they slowly move by. Tell them to imagine any thoughts going through their head as clouds. Watch their thoughts as the clouds roll by.

BREATHING BUDDIES

Have the children place a Beanie Baby on their stomach, as they lay flat on the floor. They will focus on the rise and fall of the animal as you guide them through their inhales and exhales. This will help them to bring awareness to their breath and help their mind to become focused.

SLOW MUSIC MEDITATION

Find songs that are around two to three minutes long. They could be nature sounds, like thunderstorms or rainforest noises, or sounds of the ocean. Native flutes are always nice for meditation. Have children get in a comfortable position (most will probably choose to lay down), or they can sit if that's more comfortable for them. Play the music or sound. Have them completely relax. Come out of the pose slowly after the music is over.

Meditations for Pre-Team and Team Gymnasts

Include any meditations from Chapter 3. Have the gymnasts sit in ½ Lotus, or Full Lotus if possible and their knees are stable. Practicing this pose helps to strengthen the knee and ankle joints. Three to five minutes of meditation to begin practice is a great way to shift energy from the outside world, to inside the gym, and into their bodies. If your gymnasts are completely new at meditation start them out at only a minute at a time. For a competitive athlete though you may find that one minute is way to easy though because their training already provides a primed mind. Allow meditation to make their minds even sharper! You may be able to go right into the 5 minutes.

Start simple. Nothing fancy. No bells or whistles. Just a simple five-minute seated meditation in silence. It might be hard to find a silent spot in your gym but find the quietest spot you can. Allow your team time to connect with their breath and body, letting go of anything they might be carrying with them from their day. This transition time is vital. (After meditation, move through some short warm-up poses and then into Sun Salutations or pick a few poses to continue mental preparation for the rest of your gymnastics training.)

You may find it helpful to join the team during this meditation time. Meditation is great to help you become an even better coach! You will feel more focused, organized, and energized for your team even after a short few minutes. Starting practice off this way will bring a nice centering energy into the gym, giving you a start off the the right foot. Take a few minutes in meditation before competitions as well. There's an old Zen Proverb that goes, *"You should sit in meditation everyday for 20 minutes, unless you're too busy, then you should sit for an hour."*

Warm Up Poses for All Levels

Just like we need to warm-up for gymnastics practice, or running, or any other activity to prepare the body, a few warm-up moves before we move into yoga poses is always a good idea. You can use these warm-ups to prepare the neck, wrists, ankles, and joints for all levels of gymnasts. Think of it like oiling up your car for your road trip. These simple warm up exercises are easy but profound, and will help to activate the synovial fluids in the joints.

ANKLES, WRISTS NECK ROLLS
YOGA MUDRA SEQUENCE
UNDULATING V-SEALS
CAT & COW

ANKLES/WRISTS/NECK ROLLS

Don't have them roll all at once time unless you want them to become super dizzy! J Start either at the head or feet, and move up or down. If you start with their feet, have the children sit with their legs straight out in front of them. They will bend one knee and place the outside ankle of the ankleto opposite thigh creating the number 4 with their legs. They will put one finger in between each toe and roll their ankles around carefully. The fingers in between the toes act as a nice massage and opener for the toes. After they roll their foot around at least a few times, have them give each foot a little massage. Remember how many pressure points are in our feet. Give them some lovin'! When they're done with both feet, move to circular motions in their wrists, necks, and shoulders.

YOGA MUDRA SEQUENCE

Start in a seated pretzel position. This is a sequence of four poses that will stretch and open all four sides of the spine and body. Take a moment in each step, at least a few breaths in each pose.

1. First, interlace your fingers behind you and squeeze your palms together.
2. Place your hands directly behind your body, aligned with your shoulders, and fingers pointing away from you. Lift your heart up and look up towards the sky.
3. Reach over to each side creating a rainbow shape. Press both seat bones into the floor.
4. Fold body forward and bring forearms to the floor. Back can be round. Neck is relaxed.

CAT & COW POSE

Cat & Cow is great to warm-up and activate the spine. This is a simple exercise that helps children coordinate the breath with movement. Make sure the children are doing the movements slowly and mindfully. With the synchronicity of breath and movement, the healing benefits of this pose are amazing. The mind and body are balanced. This is a great overall pose for physical, emotional, and mental stability.

UNDULATING V-SEALS

This pose combines two poses and the children will move from one yoga pose to the next as they learn to coordinate the breath with movement. From Upside Down V, as they inhale, they will move forward through Seal keeping the bottoms of the toes on ground. As they exhale they will push back into Upside Down V. Repeat three to five cycles.

Yoga for Recreational Gymnasts

The poses and yoga techniques in this section are meant to be for gymnasts just starting out in a gymnastics program. They may have little to no experience at all with gymnastics or movement. In recreational classes the kids talk more and it is harder for them to pay attention for very long. Younger kids may have a harder time focusing. Teaching them these useful skills at a younger age will help them to improve not only in gymnastics but in life.

Gymnasts that have been in the sport longer will most likely catch onto yoga a little easier. Seasoned gymnasts tend to already have gained good focus, strength and flexibility through their gymnastics practice. When teaching yoga to younger, recreational gymnasts just keep it very simple. You will add only a few breathing exercises and poses. Remind them to breathe a lot, especially in more difficult poses for them, like backbends and bridges. The poses you will do with recreational kids will be different from the ones in Chapter 6, which are more for the pre-team to team gymnasts, although you can definitely try poses you think would be good from Chapter 6. There are no limits here, simply use your best judgment based on your students.

We want to bring in imagery for younger students. Imagination can be a form of meditation since it helps to focus the mind into one direction. Imagination and imagery are probably one of the best forms of meditation you can do with younger children since it may keep their interest for a longer period of time. You can have the children pretend they are the animals while in the pose. Let them make noises and move more then you would a pre-team or team gymnast. After you lead a meditation and a few poses, if time permits, you can have each gymnast make up their own yoga poses.

The yoga poses in this section are all based on animals and nature. Children relate well to these things. Pretending to be an animal is fun for a child and encourages their imagination. Have them imagine they are an eagle in flight soaring high above the clouds, a snake slithering through the blades of grass, or a dolphin diving into the sea. Also, this will help the child to connect to animals and nature in general, something that's becoming lost in today's childhoods.

Here's a simple break down for adding yoga into recreational classes:

1. 1- Minute Meditation- have them sit in total silence.
2. 2- Minute Warm-Up Poses: Pick 2 Warm-Ups; do three times each.
3. 3- Minute Sun Salutations or Poses: 2 rounds of Sun Salutations, or pick 2-3 poses and hold for thirty seconds on each side.

If you are doing Sun Salutations with your class they will be slightly different for recreational gymnasts. Use a fun theme or story such as the example below to keep them interested. Help the child into each pose using physical adjustments as need and precise verbal cues. Overtime your gymnast's alignment and flow will get much better and you will see huge overall improvements in their focus and strength..

Let the children be creative and make up their own Sun Salutations. You could tell them how Sun Salutations were celebrated by yogis 5,000 years ago as they were used to salute the sun and each new day. Have them come up with something they can salute. Invite them to make up stories in partners, groups, or all together through the game of add on. This can make for some fun and interesting stories ☺

Sun Salutations for recreational classes:

1. **Seed Pose (Childs Pose)**
2. **Upward Salute**
3. **Forward Fold**
4. **Plank to lower all the way to floor**
5. **Seal Pose**
6. **Upside Down V**
7. **Walk feet to hands**
8. **Repeat steps 1-7 two to five times**

On the following page is an example of a fun Sun Salutation you can do with children around the ages of 3-5.

seed pose
upward salute
forward fold
plank lower down to floor
seal pose
upside down V
walk feet to hands
mountain

Have the children pretend they are seeds starting out in Seed Pose(Child's Pose) and they will grow into flowers. You can play music with rain, or use a small rain stick to make it more real for them. Have the children slowly grow tall like a flower towards the sun to Upward Salute as they take a deep breath in. From Upward Salute they will exhale and fold forward. Have then grab their ankles, shins, or the floor. Their knees will probably bend and that's ok. Have them take a moment here to shake out their necks and nodding the head yes and no. Tell them to relax and soften their facial muscles.

Next they will step both feet back into plank pose. You can have them try to hold plank with their knees up for a few seconds, then have them lower their knees to lower all the way to the ground. See if they can land their nose and belly at the same time to the ground, and have them pretend they are a bee landing on a flower. They will next inhale into Seal Pose and have them imagine they are gazing up to the sun. Have them exhale into Upside Down V Pose and pretend to be a bee eating nectar from a flower. After a couple of breaths, have them walk their feet forward to their hands. They can either inhale and circle their arms up to standing and exhale right back into forward fold to begin again, or after they inhale up to standing they can exhale to Mountain Pose.

If you'd rather practice yoga poses then Sun Salutations, the following are good asana for recreational gymnasts. Pick 2-3 poses to include into the gymnast's warm-up routine to help prepare their mind and body for practice. This few minutes will be well worth all of your time!

HORSE POSE
FROG POSE
ROCK & ROLL POSE
COBRA

HORSE POSE

Horse Pose is just like Downward Dog only you lift one of your legs straight back and up (3-legged dog). They will point all of their toes toward the floor to help level the hips. Have the children lengthen their entire body from their activated hands, all the way out their lifted and flexed heel. This pose helps to build balance and strength. Hold for at least five seconds on each side. Horse Pose helps children to find their center, helps to stimulate and balance both sides of their brain, helps to clear their minds and energize their bodies, and strengthens their arms and core.

FROG POSE

Frog Pose can be a pretty intense pose for some kids so it might be one you either save for later or try for fun and see what happens. It is a hip and thigh stretch. Have the children start on their hands and knees and bring their forearms to the ground, elbows under their shoulders. They will slow begin to walk their knees little by little out to the sides until they feel a good stretch. Have them keep their feet flexed. This will protect the knee and ankle joints. Have them find a focal point and hold or 3-5 breaths.

ROCK & ROLL POSE

Have the children rock on their backs while remaining in a tuck position. Have them hold their shins and tuck their chin towards their chest. The children will rock back and forth about five times remaining in a strong tuck position. This should feel good on their back and helps the children to gain stability and coordination. When they rock back up see if they can keep their feet from touching the floor. This pose helps builds brings strength in the core and blood flow into the spine. It also balances the mind and body.

SEAL POSE

Seal pose is just like Cobra Pose. Kids love to come into this pose and make sounds like a seal. Have them pretend they are a sleeping seal. Start by laying facing down, nose to the floor or head turned to one side. When you say, "Wake up seal", the children will raise up into the pose. When you say, "Goodnight seal", the children will return to where they started. Great for digestion, strengthens and stretches the back body, opens the heart and lungs, and much more.

V-SIT POSE
FULL WHEEL POSE
TREE POSE
AIRPLANE POSE
BUTTERFLY POSE
CHILD'S POSE

AIRPLANE POSE

Airplane Pose is like a Warrior 3 but much more playful and organic. Let the children imagine that they are like a bird or plane in flight looking out over the horizon. Arms will be out to a 'T', palms down, fingers spread, and spine as straight as possible. The can imagine they are birds or planes and have them each tell about where they are flying to.

TREE POSE

Tree Pose can have many different variations. Have the children each pretend to be trees and go around having them each say what kind of tree they are. Trees sway so if they fall or wobble remind them so. This pose is great for building balance in the body and mind, and also for building strength in the standing leg and core.

V-SIT POSE

V-Sit Pose is an advanced pose for the recreational children when done right. There are multiple versions from easy to hardest. In every variation, make sure their spines are long and strong. To start, have them keep there knees bent and hands can stay on the sides of their legs. As the children progress and get stronger, have them keep their legs straight and arms will come out to the sides, off the legs, palms up.

BUTTERFLY POSE

Have the children find a comfortable seat with seat bones equally pressing into the ground. Soles of their feet will come together as they sit up tall, shoulders are down and relaxed. They can flutter their legs a few time before coming into stillness. You can decide to have them stay here and go around in a circle having each child tell the group where they are flying to, or they can fold forward for more challenge.

FULL WHEEL POSE

Full Wheel is what you may know as a backbend if you are a gymnast. Have the children align their knees over their ankles and their shoulders over their wrists. Make sure their toes are straight forward and their feet press strong to the floor. Their fingers are spread, facing the toes, and weight is distributed evenly through all parts of the hands. Full Wheel is great for keeping their spine flexible, and body and mind healthy. If this is too difficult, your can practice Bridge Pose from Chapter 5 with them.

Yoga for Pre-Team Gymnasts

Without taking away too much time from your pre-team gymnastics practice, you can incorporate yoga concepts at the very beginning that will have lasting benefits for the rest of their practice, and potentially the rest of their lives. Pre-team gymnasts should catch onto the yoga concepts fairly easily since many parts of yoga and gymnastics are similar. Start off simple and be patient with the practice. Also the more you practice the better you will be able to understand yoga and be able to teach it. Do the meditations with them. It's good for them to see you practicing too.

You will add a little longer meditation then for the rec kids, plus the poses can be held longer. The pre-team kids may not need as much imagery in the poses and breathing exercises, due to a more mature attention span.

To get started use something like the three steps below and add on or modify as it feels right:

1. 2 to 3 Minutes- Meditation
2. 3 Minutes-Warm Up Poses: Pick 3 Warm-Ups and do three times each.
3. 5 Minutes- Sun Salutations or Poses: Three rounds of Sun Salutations, or pick three poses and hold for thirty seconds to a minute on each side.

Sun Salutations-

Any Sun Salutations from Chapter 5.

Poses-

Any poses from Chapter 6 and 7.

Yoga for Team Gymnasts

A ten to fifteen minute yoga routine at the very beginning of your team girl's practice will have lasting benefits for the rest of their practice. At first, yoga may seem boring to a competitive gymnast. It may seem too slow compared to what they are used to on a daily basis. The grind of a competitive gymnast can be brutal and intense. Yoga is very gentle, but at the same time intense (strength and surrender) because there is such an extreme amount of awareness and concentration going into each subtle movement. All parts of the whole working together, consuming ever bit of focus and concentration, in turn building focus and concentration. Focus and concentration can also be look at as muscles. The more you use them the stronger they become.

Here is a sample formula you can use to create a team warm-up yoga practice:

1. 3-5- Minute Meditation.
2. 5- Minute Warm-Up Poses Pick 3 Warm-Ups and do three times each.
3. 5- Minute Sun Salutations or Poses: Three rounds of Sun Salutations, or pick three poses and hold for one minute on each side.

Sun Salutations-

Any Sun Salutations from Chapter 5.

Poses-

Any poses from Chapter 6 and 7.

Some gymnasts will quickly understand of yoga. For other gymnasts, it may take a bit longer. A gymnast is not used to moving slow. The slower pace of yoga helps unite the gymnasts with the understanding of their body. Yoga is the study of the body. Yoga takes you deep within ourselves to the depths of our soul. Help to give this gift to your gymnasts, they will treasure it for a lifetime. Give the gift of yoga to yourself!

Start off slowly. Learn a little each day, practice one or two poses out of this book everyday, and in no time you will find your inner yogi. Yoga makes us step back and take a look at ourselves. Do you realize we see reflections of ourselves in every person we meet? If we can change the way we think, breath, and are, the things we look at change. Yoga offers so much more then a flexible body and toned abs. What you will find is more then you ever could've imagined with just a little practice each day- attitude shifts, bad habits dying, clearer thinking, more energy, and so much more! There are superstars within your and your gym just waiting to be discovered!

Still confused by how to get started with yoga? Simply begin by taking the deepest breath you've ever taken... Then do that again, and again, until you feel the weight of the world begin to melt away from you, until your mind begins to settle, until you feel back home to your true authentic self. This is yoga. You see, yoga is not the action of touching your toes, it is the action of touching something way deeper. So often we are asleep with open eyes, wandering aimlessly around from day to day. Yoga relights our path so that it becomes a little clearer, a little brighter, and a whole lot better. It becomes better not only for yourself but for the rest of the world because our lives all ripple out to each others. We are all connected.

May you find your true North and let the river carry you there...

Thank you for your practice because what we heal in ourselves we heal in the world, and so the world thanks you too!

XO, Jill Fox

BOOK REFERENCES:

HOW TO TRAIN A WILD ELEPHANT- JAN CHOZEN BAYS
LIGHT ON PRANAYAMA- IYENGAR
THE POWER OF NOW- ECKHART TOLLE
INNER TRADITION YOGA- MICHAEL STONE
THE YOGA SUTRAS OF PANTANJALI- SRI SWAMI SATCHIDANANDA
MEDITATIONS FROM THE MAT- ROLF GATES
THE SIVANANDA COMPANION TO YOGA- LUCY LIDELL
THE HEART OF YOGA- T. K. V. DESIKACHAR
THE BOOK OF MEDITATIONS FOR CHILDREN- MAUREEN GARTH
MINDFULNESS YOGA- FRANK JUDE BOCCIO
COACHING YOUTH GYMNASTICS- ASEP with USA GYMNASTICS

WEB REFERENCES:

WIKIPEDIA
SUNWARRIOR.COM
FOODANDWINE.COM
CUESA.ORG
MINDBODYGREEN.COM
WHFOODS.COM
SIMPLEGREENSMOOTHIES.COM
IDEALPHYSICALTHERAPY.COM
IDEALPHYSICALTHERAPY.COM
STYLECRAZE.COM
LEFTBRAINBUDDHA.COM
CHAKRAS.INFO
YOGATODAY.COM
GAIAM TV
WWW.FOXYSLEOS.COM

About the Author

Jill Fox lives the best of both worlds in Michigan and California with her beautiful daughter, Izabel Fox. Besides yoga and gymnastics Jill enjoys hikes, road trips, traveling, good food music, and movies! She is partial business owner of her family's business, Foxy's Leotards, in Grand Rapids, Michigan. Follow her blog at www.foxysleos.com.

Growing up a competitive elite gymnast gave Jill a passion for life, and a fascination with body and movement. In 2009 she took her Yoga Teacher Training at Mount Madonna Institute in Santa Cruz, California. Seeking to maintain her strength and flexibility from gymnastics as she aged, she was surprised to find that yoga offers so much more!

Jill has taught in many yoga studios but finds her favorite places to teach yoga are in everyday places such as gymnastics clubs, corporate offices, drug rehab & therapy centers, schools, and the beach! She knows blending yoga with a gymnastics practice will be a game changer for the sport for sure because of the focus, alignment, and confidence yoga offers. She uses many centering practices offered in this book herself and when coaching her gymnasts.

About the Editor

Always a mama first. Amber is the founder of Mindful Vinyasa School of Yoga™, the creator of Healthy Mamas™, and the author of Mindful Mama, Moments of Pause for Mothers. She is also a founding member of The Body Mind Being Project. She resides in West Michigan with her husband, two sons, and some four legged friends. Learn more about Amber at www. Amberkilpatrick.com

Made in the USA
San Bernardino, CA
07 July 2016